"Screenwriters seeking to expand their narrati
the Master. J. M. Evenson, in her cogent, acc
Bard for those essential principles that powe
characters in ways that are especially applicable to movies. Far more is shared between
stage and screen than separates them. Kudos to Evenson for a truly original contribu-
tion to this increasingly overcrowded field."

— Richard Walter, Professor and Screenwriting Chairman, UCLA School of Film

"The shrewdest and most useful screenwriting book I've found in years — it's like
having the Bard himself as your writing partner."

— Michael Colleary, writer of *Face/Off*, *Lara Croft: Tomb Raider*, and *Firehouse Dog*

"If you think Shakespeare has no relevance to contemporary filmmaking, you aren't
looking very closely. There is an unbroken line between his work and the best films
that appear this year at your local theaters. J. M. Evenson's book succinctly and vividly
looks at the writing techniques in Shakespeare's plays that can be seen at work in the
most memorable American films. An excellent, concise book!"

— Howard Suber, Professor, UCLA School of Film, and author of *The Power of Film*

"*Shakespeare for Screenwriters* offers golden lessons that can make us all better writers —
no matter what you're working on."

— Susan Hurwitz Arneson, writer on *South Park* and *Malibu Country*

"Don't re-invent the wheel — learn from the masters! Few would dispute that
Shakespeare is one of the greatest writers in history. Evenson does an excellent job
analyzing his most famous plays and explaining how to apply their lessons to
modern-day screenwriting."

— Marx H. Pyle, producer/co-host, GenreTainment;
director/creator, Reality On Demand

"An instant favorite. Concise, focused, full of fresh insights, written in an easy,
conversational style, *Shakespeare for Screenwriters* is a book that will be immensely useful
not only to practicing writers, but to teachers of Shakespeare as well. The premise is
so obvious (What practical lessons can screenwriters learn from the greatest dramatic
writer in history?) that it seems a wonder no one has done this before — but it is
deceptively difficult to distill Shakespeare's plays down to their essence, given their
complexity and the barriers of language and time. Evenson has done so with verve
and clarity: she mines each of fifteen major plays for a specific lesson in character
and structure, draws astute (and often surprising) comparisons with classic and
contemporary films, and ends each chapter with useful, practical exercises for the
working writer. In a field rife with repetitive how-to books, Evenson has come up
with an original, must-read approach on a par with Chris Vogler's *The Writer's Journey*."

— Robin Russin, writer of *On Deadly Ground*, author of *Screenplay: Writing the
Picture*, and Director of the MFA Program at UC, Riverside

"All the world's a stage, and this is the book you need in your library, whether you're a screenwriter, novelist, playwright, filmmaker, or just want to understand how Shakespeare managed to write such wonderful stories and create those fabulous characters! I love *Shakespeare for Screenwriters!*"

— Elizabeth English, Founder & Executive Director of the Moondance International Film Festival

"Sprinkled liberally with the many shining examples created by his intelligence and understanding of human nature and behavior, William Shakespeare, in his array of great plays, lays the groundwork for all writers of drama, comedy, and tragedy to emulate. No easy task because of his superior use of language, intent, emotion, force, and the motivations revealed in his characters, good and evil. J. M. Evenson parses this larder of Shakespearian dramatic treasure, peeling back layers of complexity to find revealed the kernels of truth seen in contemporary work diligently following the trails Shakespeare blazed. *Shakespeare for Screenwriters* is a splendid touchstone for all serious screenwriters, with ample examples hinged to Shakespeare's great plays."

— Fred G. Thorne writer, producer, director, professor

"This book is so much fun it makes you wonder how Shakespeare wrote all those plays without reading this first."

— Chad Gervich, writer on *Dog With a Blog* and *After Lately*, author of *Small Screen, Big Picture*

"An outstanding book. Writing, directing, acting — I've done it all, and I can tell you from experience, absolutely everybody could use a little touch of Shakespeare in their work, and this book tells you exactly how to do it!"

— Yule Caise, writer on *Heroes*

"The idea to use probably the most famous, most enduring and most popular writer of all time to explore screenwriting is absolutely inspired, but don't think you'll be mired in ancient texts with this book. Evenson deftly breaks apart the Bard's techniques for creating some of the most powerful characters, dramatic plots, and classic themes ever written and expertly focuses that lens to a host of contemporary films in a way that will improve any screenwriter's understanding of what makes great writing."

— Robert Grant, editor Sci Fi London; author of *Writing the Science Fiction Film*

"Jennie Evenson has taken the screenwriting 'how to' book to a whole new level. Through analysis of Shakespeare's work from a writer's perspective, Ms. Evenson helps to show today's writer what makes his works so gripping, then shows you how to capture their power in your own work. By looking at the great works of the past, she has paved a new road for writers to create, expand, and understand their work. 'To be, or not to be?' This book *is*."

— Timothy Albaugh, writer of *Trading Favors* and Director of Hollins University Graduate Screenwriting Program

TIMELESS WRITING TIPS FROM
the Master of Drama

SHAKESPEARE
FOR SCREENWRITERS

J. M. Evenson

Published by Michael Wiese Productions
12400 Ventura Blvd. #1111
Studio City, CA 91604
tel. 818.379.8799
fax 818.986.3408
mw@mwp.com
www.mwp.com

Cover design: Johnny Ink www.johnnyink.com
Book design: Gina Mansfield Design
Copy editor: Matt Barber

Printed by McNaughton & Gunn, Inc., Saline, Michigan
Manufactured in the United States of America

Library of Congress Cataloging-in-Publication Data

Evenson, J. M.
  Shakespeare for screenwriters : timeless writing tips from the master of
drama / J. M. Evenson.
     p. cm.
  ISBN 978-1-61593-141-5
  1. Motion picture authorship--Vocational guidance. 2. Shakespeare, William, 1564-1616--Technique. I. Title.
  PN1996.E94 2013
  808.2'3--dc23
                                        2013004682

Printed on recycled stock
Publisher plants ten trees for every one tree used to produce this book.

TABLE OF CONTENTS

ACKNOWLEDGMENTS

This book could not have been completed without the thoughtful insights and kind enthusiasm of my esteemed friends and fellow writers Austin Formato, Barbara Curry, Paul Taegel, Yule Caise, Maureen Johnson, and Marshall Thornton. I'd also like to thank the publishers, Michael Wiese and Ken Lee, for their unflagging support for this project.

Most of all, I'd like to offer my heartfelt gratitude to my wonderful husband, Attila, and our beautiful children. In the words of Shakespeare, my love for you is richer than my tongue.

INTRODUCTION

What can screenwriters learn from Shakespeare?

"To be, or not to be? That is the question."

Millions of people worldwide recognize these lines from William Shakespeare's *Hamlet*. They're part of one of the greatest masterpieces in the English language. They've captivated our imaginations for hundreds of years. And they're spoken by a character whose intricate psychological complexities continue to intrigue us.

Each year there are thousands of stage productions of Shakespeare's plays worldwide. His unique creative genius transcends barriers of language, culture, time, and place. Love, family, power, war — these are the issues Shakespeare addresses. His plays touch a nerve because they are raw, human, and utterly timeless.

Every writer on Earth wishes that they could create a character like Hamlet or a love story like *Romeo and Juliet*. But how did Shakespeare create characters of such compelling psychological depth? What makes his stories so romantic, funny, heartrending, or terrifying? Why has his work stood the test of time? In short, what is the magic of Shakespeare?

Shakespeare for Screenwriters analyzes Shakespeare from a writer's perspective, breaking down famous stories, scenes, and characters in Shakespeare's greatest works to discover what makes them so gripping — and then shows you how to capture their power in your own screenplays. In the process, the book reveals powerful storytelling secrets from the one of the greatest writers who ever lived.

Unlocking the secret to Shakespeare's magic is, of course, no easy task. So how are we going to do it? Each chapter focuses on three specific lessons that can be learned from Shakespeare, showing you how to translate the power of Shakespeare's dramatic devices to the big screen. Focusing on powerful moments in film, each chapter illustrates the lessons we can learn from Shakespeare with clear examples from some of the best movies of our time.

In one chapter, for instance, we dissect the obsessive ambition of Lady Macbeth — and then, to see how her unyielding passion might translate to the silver screen, we look at one of the most haunting portraits of raw ambition ever committed to film: cult favorite *Scarface* (1983). The point is not to argue that *Scarface* was written as an homage to Shakespeare. Clearly, it wasn't. Yet, the movie provides an excellent example of how this one particular dramatic device can work in modern film.

The end of each chapter provides a list of movies to watch, as well as three writing exercises designed to help you uncover timeless themes, stories, and characters in your own stories. The goal is simple: take the respected wisdom of Shakespeare and turn it into practical writing advice for you. If you're going to study writing, why not learn from the very best?

Shakespeare's influence on Hollywood has been profound. Many of the greatest filmmakers of our time, from Orson Welles to Joss Whedon, have been so intrigued by Shakespeare's work that they've produced Hollywood movies of his plays. Even more have used Shakespeare's narratives as the underlying structure of indirect adaptations. Rather than focusing on adaptations or the scholarly pursuit of tracking down cinematic references, however, this book uncovers storytelling techniques in Shakespeare's work and shows you how to incorporate those techniques into your own screenplays.

Some readers might worry that they haven't read enough Shakespeare. Most of us read a play or two in high school or college, but few of us are experts. You absolutely do not need to be an expert to read this book — it's geared to all levels of interest and experience in both Shakespeare and screenwriting. Each chapter reminds you of the biggest moments in the plays and goes through each scene step-by-step. In addition, an appendix summarizing the main plot of each play has been included at the back of the book. And, of course, there are plenty of online sources should you wish to explore even further. The point isn't to turn anyone into a Shakespeare scholar, but rather to lay out the practical writing lessons we can learn from "The Bard" in clear, concise terms.

If you've ever wondered what makes Shakespeare's writing so special, and wished you could add a little bit of that magic into your own work, this book is for you. Shakespeare wrote the most powerful dramas, comedies, romances, thrillers, and historical epics in the English language. *Shakespeare for Screenwriters* tells you how.

PART I

THE
GREAT
PLAYS

Chapter One

HAMLET

"To thine own self be true":
Creating psychological depth in your characters.

OF ALL SHAKESPEARE'S PLAYS, by far the most frequently performed, quoted, and referenced, is *Hamlet*. Thousands of stage performances take place every year, and more than fifty film adaptations of the drama have been produced since 1900. *Hamlet* is, without a doubt, the cornerstone of Western literature and culture.

Why are actors, directors, critics, and readers drawn to this text? Why is the play so important?

The central innovation of this play is the character of Hamlet himself. He is smart, introspective, angry, despondent, euphoric, nostalgic, witty, and possibly mad. Like a prism, his character reveals a rainbow of emotions. Audiences are drawn-in almost as if they are solving a puzzle. How did Shakespeare create a character with such compelling psychological depth? How can we build this complexity into our own characters?

BUILD INNER CONFLICT

The key to building complexity into your characters is giving them an important decision, and then making the arguments for and against it equally strong. Watching a character struggle with inner conflict generates sympathy and creates psychological depth that audiences recognize as uniquely human.

For Hamlet, the struggle begins in the very first pages. Hamlet, the Prince of Denmark, is visited by the Ghost of his father, the former king. The Ghost reveals to Hamlet that he was murdered by Claudius, the now-reigning king, and demands that Hamlet kill Claudius in revenge.

If Hamlet were a typical avenger, he would go do it. But Hamlet is a thinker. What if the Ghost is lying? What if it's the devil in disguise? What if Hamlet's own mind is playing tricks on him? What would happen to Hamlet's soul if he kills the wrong guy? Hamlet is consumed by doubt. In a moment of pure anguish, he asks his famous question:

> *To be, or not to be? That is the question:*
> *Whether 'tis nobler in the mind to suffer*
> *The slings and arrows of outrageous fortune,*
> *Or to take arms against a sea of troubles,*
> *And by opposing end them?* (Act 3, scene 1)

In this passage, we discover the true nature of Hamlet's dilemma. It's not just about whether or not Hamlet should kill Claudius, it's about the nature of life and death. Why do bad things happen to us? Is it better to die than to suffer? What happens to us after death? These are real questions — ones that humanity has struggled with since the dawn of time. The directive from the Ghost thrusts Hamlet into a moral quandary, and from that moment on, Hamlet is ripped apart by an agonizing internal conflict. Should he, or shouldn't he, kill Claudius?

Audiences love watching characters be torn apart by inner conflict. Take the character of Jim Stark in *Rebel Without a Cause* (1955), for instance. We watch Jim (James Dean) battle both his inner demons and the treacherous world around him. As he tries to cope with local bully Buzz and his gang, Jim looks to his father for help. Over and over again, Jim asks his father: "What can you do when you have to be a man?" The question becomes central in the most famous scene, when Buzz forces Jim to play a game of "chicken" in a drag race. Jim knows it's a dangerous game, but if he doesn't play, how can he be a man? When Buzz's jacket gets caught on the handle of his car door, accidentally dragging him over the cliff to an explosive death, Jim goes into an emotional tailspin. His anguished guilt erupts when he screams out the celebrated line: "You're tearing me apart!"

MAKE UNEXPECTED CHOICES

Every writer knows that characters are the sum of their choices. What we sometimes forget is that audiences love to watch characters make unexpected choices. The choices your characters make should surprise, provoke, and intrigue the audience.

Hamlet is faced with a serious decision when he finds Claudius alone and unguarded in a church. As far as Hamlet can tell, Claudius is praying. The question is whether or not to seize the moment and kill Claudius on the spot:

> *Now might I do it pat, now he is praying;*
> *And now I'll do't. And so he goes to heaven;*
> *And so am I revenged?*
> *...O, this is hire and salary, not revenge!* (Act 3, scene 3)

Despite the fact that it's the perfect opportunity to act, Hamlet sheathes his sword and walks away. Why doesn't he just do it? The unexpected choice is curious, at first. But Hamlet argues that if it's only "hire and salary," then that makes him no better than a common mercenary. If it's mercenary work, then he could be sending Claudius to heaven while damning his own soul. The stakes are suddenly no longer about the here and now, but about eternal damnation. Even if Hamlet knew for certain that Claudius killed his father, would it really be a good idea to murder him in a church, of all places?

Hamlet can't hear him, but Claudius *isn't* actually praying in the scene. Claudius whispers to the audience that he killed Hamlet's father so that he could sleep with Gertrude, Hamlet's mother. He isn't even sorry he did it! As Hamlet walks away, the audience knows Hamlet has made a mistake, but the choice is intriguingly complex and leaves the audience on edge. Will this foul murderer get away with it?

Unexpected choices are at the heart of *Good Will Hunting* (1997). Like Hamlet, Will (Matt Damon) also makes decisions that are, at first, deeply curious. When Professor Lambeau sets up interviews at high-powered companies to help Will better himself, Will deliberately flubs the interviews — even going so far as to make a mockery of the companies by sending his uneducated best friend to taunt them. Then, when Skylar tells him that she loves him and wants him to come with her to California, Will lies and says that he doesn't love her. What we learn from Will's unexpected choices is that he doesn't want to let anyone help him. He keeps everything good in life at arm's length because he doesn't trust it. In the most famous scene, therapist Sean Maguire (Robin Williams) recounts a story to Will. Sean had tickets to the historic sixth game of the 1975 World Series, which the Boston Red Sox won — but Sean gave up those tickets to "go see about a girl." It was an unexpected choice, but not one he regrets. Sean's story becomes important in the final scene of the movie, when Will finally makes a good decision. He thanks Lambeau for the job opportunities but decides to "go see about a girl" — then takes off cross country to find the woman he loves.

Good Will Hunting, ©1997 Lionsgate, All Rights Reserved.

Unexpected choices draw audiences in. The more intriguing the choice, the more we feel compelled to watch the character and find out why they did it. At every point, unexpected choices must be organic to character, revealing a fundamental truth about that character's nature.

LET YOUR CHARACTERS STRUGGLE AND GROW

When we compare Hamlet to Laertes, the other character in the play who loses his father, a striking difference emerges. After Hamlet kills Polonius, Laertes' father, Claudius asks Laertes if he would like to avenge his father's death by killing Hamlet. Without skipping a beat, Laertes replies that he would "cut his throat i' the church." The lines recall Hamlet's refusal to kill Claudius while he is praying in the church. If Hamlet is beset with more questions than answers, Laertes is his exact opposite. Laertes is a simple character, untroubled by philosophical questions of should or would. At no point in the play does Laertes grow or change; he takes revenge as his one objective, and he does it. As a result, Laertes is psychologically flat, because we never see him struggle to find the answers. Part of psychological depth is watching our characters struggle and grow.

One of the greatest portraits of struggle and change is the character of Terry Malloy in *On The Waterfront* (1954). The movie begins with Terry (Marlon Brando) coaxing dockworker Joey Doyle out of his apartment into an ambush. Joey dies, preventing him from testifying against Johnny Friendly, the mob union boss who controls the docks. Things get complicated, however, when Terry meets, and falls in love with, Edie, Joey's sister. As guilt over Joey's death eats away at him, Terry increasingly leans toward testifying against the big mob boss. By the end of the movie, Terry changes sides completely. Far from the henchman he started out as, Terry becomes a symbol of resistance when he is attacked and viciously beaten by Friendly's thugs. The longshoremen rally around Terry in the final confrontation, refusing to work unless Terry works, too. Bruised and battered, Terry drags himself onto the dock, taking charge as the new leader. Through the course of the movie, we watch Terry wrestle with his awakening conscience. His remarkable transformation offers a glimpse inside the character by being part of his change — and the result is that we both understand and care about him.

Many screenwriting manuals will tell you to find a single motivation and make sure your character stays on point. But what we learn from *Hamlet, Rebel Without a Cause, Good Will Hunting*, and *On The Waterfront*, is that sometimes it's better to not limit your characters to one motivation that remains stable through the course of the story. Let your characters struggle with their inner conflicts. Let them unfold before us as they grow and change throughout the course of the story.

Key Points to Remember

† Watching characters struggle with inner conflict generates empathy for the character and creates psychological complexity.

† To build inner conflict, give your characters an important decision and then make the arguments for and against it equally strong.

† Have your characters make unexpected choices that surprise, provoke, or intrigue the audience.

† Allowing your characters to struggle and grow over the course of the story helps to create a sense of psychological depth.

Movies to Watch

On The Waterfront (1954)
Rebel Without a Cause (1955)
Good Will Hunting (1997)

Exercises

I.   Think of some of the hardest decisions you've had to make. What were the reasons for and against your decision? How did you decide what to do? Create a character around one particular decision. List all the reasons why they should, and shouldn't, do it — making both cases equally strong. Then write a two-page scene in which that character is forced to make a decision.

2. List your top three favorite characters on film. What decisions were they forced to make? Were they conflicted about these decisions? What effect did it have on their character?

3. Make a character grow and change. Think of who you want your character to be at the end of the story. Then choose character traits that are the direct opposite of who you want the character to become — this is who they are at the beginning. How must the character grow and change to achieve the traits you want them to have at the end? What will the character need to do to acquire the necessary traits?

Chapter Two

ROMEO AND JULIET

"Parting is such sweet sorrow":
Climaxes should be inevitable (but not predictable).

*R*OMEO AND JULIET IS GENERALLY REGARDED as the most tragic of all Shakespeare's plays. Telling the heartrending story of two lovers torn apart by feuding families, the play has a uniquely affecting power.

Most people believe it is the sweet tale of young love that makes this play so tragic. But consider this: would we feel the same about this play if Romeo and Juliet lived to get old and bicker? The spectacular final sequence, in which both Romeo and Juliet take their own lives, is the real heart of the play. It is the inevitable end to a perfect love.

That sense of inevitability is, in fact, the key to the play's magic. The climax of *Romeo and Juliet* achieves its poignancy because it feels as if it couldn't have ended any other way. How does Shakespeare craft that sense of inevitability? How does he keep the ending from seeming predictable? What lessons can we learn for writing our own climactic endings?

FORETELLING

In the first few lines of *Romeo and Juliet*, Shakespeare does something unexpected: he gives away the ending of the play. In fact, the lines lay out the entire plot of the play, telling the audience in no uncertain terms that Romeo and Juliet will fall in love and die:

Two households, both alike in dignity,
In fair Verona, where we lay our scene,
From ancient grudge break to new mutiny,

Where civil blood makes civil hands unclean.
From forth the fatal loins of these two foes
A pair of star-cross'd lovers take their life;
Whose misadventured piteous overthrows
Do with their death bury their parents' strife. (Act I, scene I)

Shakespeare is using a powerful literary device called *foretelling*. Fore-telling (also called *prolepsis*) is a flash forward in the action, in which we learn what is going to happen at the end of the story. While it seems counterintuitive to give away the story, the lines actually pique our interest: from the first lines in the play, the audience knows they are in for a deliciously gory tale of sex, violence, and death — and it sounds good.

The fact that Shakespeare gives away so much brings us to a valuable lesson: many writers are afraid that setting up the climax with foretelling will spoil the surprise. But this is not the case. If we look at a movie like *American Beauty* (1999), for instance, we see that foretelling does nothing to diminish the shock of the climax. The film begins with a voiceover, the modern equivalent of a chorus:

My name is Lester Burnham. This is my neighborhood; this is my street; this is my life. I am 42 years old. Within a year I will be dead.

Even after we hear this, do we know that Lester's ex-paramilitary neighbor will mistake Lester for a gay man, try to seduce him, and then shoot Lester in the head? Foretelling doesn't ruin the end; instead, it lends significance to every move Lester makes because we know that he will die — and soon.

Foretelling has, in fact, become a popular device in modern cinema. *Sunset Boulevard* (1950) starts with the dead body of the protagonist floating in the pool; more recently, the animated feature *Megamind* (2010) begins with the main character falling to his death. Cutting across time and genre, foretelling is a powerful dramatic device. Rather than quashing intrigue, it makes the audience more curious about the character and their journey. The joy of the story becomes less about *what* will happen, and more about *how* and *why*.

Foreshadowing

Foreshadowing is a system of signs that seem like obvious clues in retrospect. Its purpose is to give the audience a window into what is coming. It is, quite literally, a shadow of the future.

Shakespeare weaves foreshadowing into every act of *Romeo and Juliet*, strategically placing it at momentous events in the lives of the characters. When Juliet first sees Romeo, the first words she speaks are to the Nurse, asking who Romeo is:

> *Go ask his name: if he be married,*
> *My grave is like to be my wedding bed.* (Act 1, scene 2)

In that crucial moment when Juliet first sees Romeo, her first thought is of death. And it is not the last time she talks about it. Just before they consummate their marriage, Juliet opines:

> *Give me my Romeo; and, when he shall die,*
> *Take him and cut him out in little stars,*
> *And he will make the face of heaven so fine*
> *That all the world will be in love with night*
> *And pay no worship to the garish sun.* (Act 3, scene 2)

As Romeo leaves, she looks down at him from the balcony and says:

> *O God, I have an ill divining soul!*
> *Methinks I see thee now, thou art so low,*
> *As one dead in the bottom of a tomb.*
> *Either my eyesight fails me, or thou lookest pale.* (Act 3, scene 5)

Perhaps the most telling instance of foreshadowing, however, is Juliet's faked death in Act 4, which acts as a preview for the final scenes. Juliet has already been "dead" once; by the time we get to the final scene, her demise seems inevitable.

Throughout the course of the story, Shakespeare refers to death over and over again. The references have a specific purpose here: to tell the audience what is coming. Even though the audience knows Romeo and Juliet are going to die, we hope against hope that they won't. The tragedy is how close they come to triumph.

THE TWIST

By the end, Romeo and Juliet's death is inevitable. But even with all the foreshadowing, previews, and considerations of death, the audience still could not predict the *exact* way the ending would happen. We could not predict that Juliet's letter to Romeo explaining her fake death would go missing; or that Romeo would show up while Juliet was still under the potion; or that Romeo, thinking Juliet is dead, would kill himself, only to have Juliet wake up moments later and kill herself, too. Shakespeare's climactic ending is a twisty, complex machine of surprises and terrors. It is a perfect combination of foretelling, foreshadowing, and twists — and it leads to an ending that is inevitable, but not predictable.

For those of you still convinced that foreshadowing will give away the ending, let's take a closer look at the thriller genre. Thrillers are supposed to scare, shock, and puzzle us with their mysteries. While those scares would seem to depend on complete surprise, one of the most terrifying movies of all time, *The Shining* (1980), makes liberal use of foreshadowing. The foreshadowing doesn't ruin the surprise — it intensifies it.

When Jack Torrance (Jack Nicholson) is first offered the winter caretaker job at the Overlook Hotel, his boss warns him about the dangers of snow-bound isolation, recounting the story of the last winter caretaker, who went nuts and butchered his family. Rather than keeping the gruesome story a mystery, we learn this within the first few scenes of the movie. This piece of foreshadowing lets us know that Jack and his family are in danger. The result is that we are scared for them right from the beginning.

The foreshadowing doesn't end there. In scene after scene, we get pieces of information that reveal the perils ahead. Just before they leave for Overlook, we see Wendy, Jack's wife, tell her friend that Jack once dislocated their son Danny's arm. Then, just after they get there, we see Jack wake from a terrible dream:

> JACK: *I had the most terrible nightmare I ever had. It's the most horrible dream I ever had.*
> WENDY: *It's okay, it's okay now. Really.*

JACK: *I dreamed that I killed you and Danny. But I didn't just kill you. I cut you up in little pieces. Oh my God. I must be losing my mind.*

Clearly, the dream is meant to both recall the warning from Stuart and tell us about what is to come: Jack will lose his mind and try to chop both Wendy and Danny to pieces. Rather than diffusing tension, the information audiences receive in foreshadowing acts like Alfred Hitchcock's proverbial "bomb under the table": it builds suspense. We wait with fear and dread for the climactic sequence to explode on stage — and when it does, it is terrifying.

As with *Romeo and Juliet*, there is no way the audience could predict the exact way the ending of *The Shining* would happen. The final scenes include twist after twist, building to one of the most frightening climactic sequences on film. Who can forget the moment when Jack Nicholson axes his way through the door, screaming: "Wendy! I'm home!"? The ending is shocking, thrilling — and unpredictable.

The Shining, ©1980 Warner Bros., All Rights Reserved.

What we can learn from these examples is that foretelling and foreshadowing are effective ways to heighten tragedy and boost suspense. Because the audience knows, to some extent, what's in store for them, the ending feels inevitable. Making sure the final sequence is full of shocking twists prevents the climax from becoming predictable.

KEY POINTS TO REMEMBER

† *Foretelling* (a flash forward in the action) and foreshadowing (clues to what will happen) are crucial tools for setting up your climax.

† Setting up the ending with foretelling and foreshadowing is the key to creating a fitting end to your story.

† Foreshadowing and foretelling won't ruin the surprise of the ending — they intensify it.

† Giving the ending a satisfying twist keeps it from feeling predictable.

MOVIES TO WATCH

Sunset Boulevard (1950)
The Shining (1980)
American Beauty (1999)
Megamind (2010)

EXERCISES

1. Re-watch your favorite movie, paying close attention to how the climax is set up. What tools does the filmmaker use? Can you find instances of foretelling or foreshadowing? What effect does it have on the story?

2. Create a short story around a climax, setting up what will happen in the end first. Write a two-page outline for a story starting with the climax and then moving toward the beginning. How does this change your experience of storytelling? How does it affect the story?

3. If you are currently working on a script, take another look at your outline. How does your story end? Have you set up the ending in acts one, two, and three? Can you find ways to use foreshadowing or foretelling to increase the tension? Have you added a twist to your ending?

Chapter Three

MACBETH

"Out, damned spot!":
Why we love obsessed characters.

OF ALL SHAKESPEARE'S FEMALE CHARACTERS, by far the most captivating is Lady Macbeth. Though the play is named after her husband, Macbeth, it is actually her unyielding ambition, not his, that plunges them into a plot to kill the king and take over the throne of Scotland. She is the one who drives the action of the play, from the multiple murders to the cover-up. Lady Macbeth is the fanatical center of this bloody play — the essence of all-consuming obsession.

Audiences love obsessed characters. They are gritty, goal-oriented, indomitable — and *fun* to watch. Their passionate energy magnetizes everyone around them, including the audience.

Exactly how does Lady Macbeth's obsession work? How can we translate that obsession to the screen?

START OFF STRONG

The first time we meet Lady Macbeth, she has just received a letter from her husband recounting a prophecy that he will become king. Lady Macbeth doesn't stop to think; she immediately hatches a plan to kill the reigning king, Duncan:

Come, you spirits
That tend on mortal thoughts, unsex me here,
And fill me from the crown to the toe top-full
Of direst cruelty! Make thick my blood;
Stop up the access and passage to remorse,
That no compunctious visitings of nature
Shake my fell purpose, nor keep peace between

> *The effect and it! Come to my woman's breasts,*
> *And take my milk for gall, you murdering ministers,*
> *Wherever in your sightless substances*
> *You wait on nature's mischief!* (Act I, scene 5)

From the moment she opens her mouth, Lady Macbeth burns with the passion that will propel the whole play. She's not only ready to kill, she's ready to call on dark forces, the "murdering ministers," to help out. But this isn't even what's unsettling about the passage. Lady Macbeth hopes to be unsexed — either to be made into a man, or into something altogether unnatural — so that she can pursue this course of "direst cruelty." Lady Macbeth's introduction crackles with energy, and we know we're in for a wild ride.

The introduction of your character is crucial in every script. With obsessed characters, we need to see that they are willing to do anything from the first moment. Take the harrowing depiction of Daniel Plainview in *There Will Be Blood* (2007). When we first meet Daniel (Daniel Day-Lewis), he's mining silver ore at the bottom of a shaft. As he begins to climb, hefting his load of ore, the ladder breaks. He plummets to the bottom of the shaft, breaking his leg. But he does not give up. He drags himself up the broken ladder, and then all the way into town, to sell the ore. We know in that moment that he is obsessed with money, and nothing will stop him. We know that there will be blood — and it is terrifying.

BE AUDACIOUS

Macbeth resists his wife's plan to kill Duncan, launching a series of protests. In retaliation, Lady Macbeth unleashes a searing attack that begins with an assault on his manhood ("Are you a man?") and ends with a horrific declaration of resolve:

> *I have given suck, and know*
> *How tender 'tis to love the babe that milks me:*
> *I would, while it was smiling in my face,*
> *Have pluck'd my nipple from his boneless gums,*
> *And dash'd the brains out, had I so sworn as you*
> *Have done to this.* (Act I, scene 7)

The images in this speech are shocking. What kind of mother could rip a smiling infant from her breast and bash its head against a wall? Nevertheless, her arguments prove persuasive: by the end of the scene, Macbeth agrees to murder Duncan. The power of her obsession allows her to control everyone around her — including her husband, the would-be king. But what's truly frightening about Lady Macbeth is her audacity. She is willing to do the unthinkable. Her ruthlessness startles both her husband and the audience.

Obsessed characters must show that they are different from everyone around them. We want to see the intensity of their desire, and we want them to shock us. Consider the depiction of Annie Wilkes in the movie *Misery* (1990). Who can forget the scene where Annie (Kathy Bates) straps the author to a bed and takes a sledgehammer to his ankle? The sequence is as terrifying as it is unforgettable. The chilling act, in all its demented audacity, frightens us into believing that her obsession is like no other. She is, and will always be, the author's "number one fan."

SPIRAL INTO INSANITY

At no point does Lady Macbeth show any kind of compunction for murdering Duncan. In fact, she spends most of her time making fun of her husband for being weak. But in the final sequence, she unravels in one spectacular scene:

Out, damned spot! Out, I say! One, two: why,
then, 'tis time to do't. Hell is murky! Fie, my
Lord, fie! A soldier, and afeard? What need we
Fear who knows it, when none can call our power to
Account? Yet who would have thought the old man
To have had so much blood in him. (Act 5, scene 1)

Gone completely mad, she scrubs at hands she imagines covered with blood — the psychological manifestation of her guilt. Even then, Lady Macbeth doesn't regret the blistering ambition that drove her actions. She continues to berate her husband for being "afeard." For Lady Macbeth, it isn't fear that destroys her, it is her obsession. She was willing to give up everything in herself for her one goal. Having it, and nothing else, drives her mad. Her suicide at the end marks her defeat — her just desserts self-administered with the same knife that killed Duncan.

Just as audiences love to watch obsessed characters, they love to see those characters spiral into insanity. These crazed characters give us a way to fulfill inner desires to possess, control, and dominate — a kind of vicarious thrill-ride. But we need to see them get their just desserts at the end. Their punishment confirms our fears about the nature of fixation and dangers of enterprising murder and mayhem. Their demise is part of what makes them compelling as characters: the audience knows they will be destroyed by their ambitions, and we wait for it.

Perhaps no movie has captured that moment as evocatively as *Scarface* (1983). The tale of the rise and fall of a drug-dealing Cuban immigrant is both compelling and unsettling — a haunting portrait of raw ambition. From the start, Tony Montana (Al Pacino) is consumed with the desire to make it. Unlike the small-time thugs he hangs around with, he knows what he is and what he will be:

> TONY: *I want what's coming to me.*
> MANNY: *Oh? What's coming to you?*
> TONY: *The world, chico, and everything in it.*

Tony is as good as his word. He starts out as a lowly assistant to the crime boss, Frank, but eventually takes over Frank's business, his contacts, and even his girlfriend, Elvira. On his way up, Tony ruthlessly murders one gangster after the next. Tony is unstoppable — the world is his.

Getting everything that he ever wanted, however, doesn't make Tony happy. In fact, the moment Tony realizes that he has it all is his low point in the movie. At the club, surrounded by champagne, women, and piles of cocaine, Tony rages against success:

> *Is this it? That's what it's all about, Manny? Eating, drinking, fucking, sucking? Snorting? Then what? You're 50. You got a bag for a belly. You got tits,*

you need a bra. They got hair on them. You got a liver, they got spots on it, and you're eating this fuckin' shit, looking like these rich fucking mummies in here.

The obsession that propelled him to success is gone. In its place is a terrifying abyss. The realization of his one true goal — being a kingpin — leaves Tony with nothing more to look forward to. Like Lady Macbeth, it is success, not failure, that prompts the eventual unraveling of Tony's mind.

And unravel it does. At the climax, the supplier that Tony betrayed, Sosa, has come for revenge. As Sosa's men enter the mansion, killing one guard after the next, Tony grabs his gun. In a coke-fuelled frenzy, Tony races out into the crossfire with his M16 assault rifle, uttering his famous lines: "Say hello to my little friend!" Tony is shot more than a dozen times, his life ending in bloody blaze. The final image is of Tony's tangled corpse at the foot of a marble statue that reads "The World Is Yours" — a call back to the lines Tony speaks to Manny near the beginning: "I want...the world, chico, and everything in it."

Obsessed characters are riveting to watch. We are magnetized by their shocking stories. We enjoy watching them burn with passion — and we relish their final moments as they collide with the inevitable.

Scarface, ©1983 Universal, All Rights Reserved.

KEY POINTS TO REMEMBER

† Show that your character is willing to do whatever it takes to get what they want in their introduction.

† Let the intensity of their desires shock us with its audacity.

† Audiences love to watch ambitious characters rise, but we also enjoy watching them be destroyed by their obsession at the end.

MOVIES TO WATCH

Scarface (1983)
Misery (1990)
There Will Be Blood (2007)

EXERCISES

1. Everybody has been obsessed with something at some point in their lives. Name one thing you were obsessed with, and then make a list of the top ten most shockingly audacious things you did (or wished you did!) to get it.

2. Create an obsessed character. They could be bent on anything — from taking over the local PTA to taking over the world. Make the same top ten list for this crazed character.

3. Imagine an opening scene for your hypothetical character that crackles with obsessive energy. What is your character doing? How does the scene show that your character is willing to do whatever it takes? Make it shock us with its audacity.

Chapter Four

OTHELLO

"These words are razors to my wounded heart":
The power of personal tragedies.

S HAKESPEARE'S TRAGEDIES ARE TYPICALLY SET during historically significant moments. *Hamlet* features the death of the king; *Macbeth* features the murder of the Scottish monarch; *King Lear* features the downfall of an empire.

But *Othello* does not involve the rise or fall of kingdoms, nor is it set during a time of political turmoil. It is the account of how one man ends up killing his beloved wife — a small story, by most measures. Yet, the play is remembered as one of Shakespeare's greatest tragedies. Why? What makes this play so powerful?

RAISE THE PERSONAL STAKES

Othello may at first seem different, but if we look closer we see that it shares a fundamental core with other tragedies: it makes us feel pity, fear, and sorrow. Focused on the story of two people in love, *Othello* strips away the framework of political upheaval to reveal the true heart of tragedy: emotion.

As writers, we are often tempted to build up grand frameworks around our narrative in hopes of raising the stakes. It's not just one man in trouble, it's the whole country — or better yet, it's the world that's in danger. But the true source of the tragedy is the emotional toll it takes on the characters. It is deep, intense, and intimate. It often involves a threat to someone the protagonist knows and loves. It is the personal stakes, not the grand framework, that resonate with audiences.

Consider the movie *Ordinary People* (1980). It tells the story of a family attempting to return to normal life after the drowning death of one teenage son and the attempted suicide of the surviving son. The heartrending scene in which a psychologist pushes young Conrad (Timothy Hutton) to stop blaming himself for his brother's death is painful, beautiful, terrifying, and cathartic — a virtual symphony of human emotions. The film is remembered today as one the most profound depictions of grief ever produced. It achieves this feat not through a grand framework but rather through deeply personal stakes: will this family be able to move on?

Even stories set during historically significant moments need to show the personal stakes. *Life is Beautiful* (1998), for example, focuses on one of the greatest tragedies of humankind: the Holocaust. And yet the moment we really *feel* the tragedy is the moment we see Guido (Roberto Benigni) clutching his little boy and shielding his young eyes from the massive pile of corpses stacked by the gas chamber. It's the personal connection that makes the horror real.

The best tragedies are not necessarily the ones that involve the highest political stakes. They are the ones that envelope our characters in anguish. When they suffer, we feel.

SHOW US THE LOVE

Othello opens with a profoundly personal crisis. Desdemona's father, Brabantio, wakens to discover that Othello has stolen off with his daughter, Desdemona. Furious, Brabantio drags Othello and Desdemona before the Doge, demanding an explanation. In one of the more eloquent speeches in Shakespeare's canon, Othello recounts "the round unvarnished tale" of how he would visit Desdemona and tell her fabulous stories from his swashbuckling past — stories she would drink up with "greedy ears." Peppering his speech with exquisite details, Othello argues that Desdemona fell in love with his stories, and by extension, him:

> *She loved me for the dangers I had pass'd,*
> *And I loved her that she did pity them.* (Act I, scene 3)

At the end of the speech, the Doge offers no rebuttal. He simply replies: "I think this tale would woo my daughter, too." What began as a crisis dissolves into kind words and good wishes — and all by the end of the third scene.

Opening with a resolution may seem like an unusual choice, but the question of whether or not Othello and Desdemona love each other is very much at the heart of the play. Just as importantly, by starting with the story of how they fell in love, Shakespeare offers us a glimpse of Othello and Desdemona as a happy couple. He shows us that their bond is strong, genuine, and tender. Because the tragedy in this play depends exclusively on the loss of their love, the audience needs to see how happy they were at the beginning, so we know how far they have fallen when their relationship deteriorates at the end. The more we understand the personal bonds that tie one character to another, the more we feel at the end when their bond is severed.

This is certainly true in *The Curious Case of Benjamin Button* (2008), which features the unusual romance between Daisy (Cate Blanchett) and Benjamin (Brad Pitt), who is aging in reverse. They meet when Daisy is six and Benjamin is twelve. Though Benjamin appears to be an old man, the two become fast friends. When they meet again, they are both of comparable age, and they fall in love. It is a sweet time, filled with happiness — and a child. But it must end: Daisy will only grow older, and Benjamin younger. The last time they see each other, Daisy doesn't run to Benjamin or embrace him. She coolly and calmly introduces Benjamin to the daughter he's never met as a "family friend." In that one moment, the love lost becomes painfully clear.

The Curious Case of Benjamin Button, ©2008 Paramount, All Rights Reserved.

SHOW US THE LOSS

In *Othello*, we see what is lost in one gut-wrenching scene at the end of the play. Othello, believing that Desdemona has been unfaithful, resolves to kill her. But then he stands over her sleeping body. As he kisses her lips one last time, he can't believe how beautiful and innocent she looks:

> *Be thus when thou art dead, and I will kill thee,*
> *And love thee after.* (Act 5, scene 2)

The conflict within Othello is palpable: he kisses her again and again, unable to stop himself. The strange paradox is the magic of the scene. Othello is both drawn in and repulsed by her. His feelings for Desdemona are irresolvable — and he kills her.

Just as we need to understand the bonds between characters, we need to see the moment when that bond is truly broken. This final moment between Desdemona and Othello contrasts the first scene, where their love triumphed, with their ultimate doom. It is the most crucial scene in the play because it is the moment where we see the tragedy in its fullness.

It is no mistake that the two most memorable scenes in *Titanic* (1997) follow this same pattern. At the beginning of their romance, Jack (Leonardo DiCaprio) takes Rose (Kate Winslet) to the prow of the ship. They climb up to the top, eyes closed. Then she opens her eyes and raises her arms as he holds her close in the racing wind. It is one the most romantic moments on film. The second is at the end of the movie, as Jack and Rose wait to be rescued. As the rescue boat nears, Rose turns to Jack, only to realize that he is already dead. Jack slips away to a cold, watery death. It is an unforgettable moment — a vision of true love lost. The perfect balance of these two scenes, the romance and the loss, is what makes us cry at the end. It's what makes us *feel*.

Titanic, ©1997 Paramount, All Rights Reserved.

These tragedies remind us to keep the pain close. Because tragedies prove most powerful when they are personal.

Key Points to Remember

† The true source of the tragedy is the emotional toll it takes on the characters.

† It is the personal stakes, not the grand framework, that resonate with audiences.

† The more we understand the personal bonds between characters, the more we feel when that bond is threatened.

† Just as we need to understand the bonds between characters, we need to see the moment when that bond is truly broken.

Movies to Watch

Ordinary People (1980)
Titanic (1997)
Life is Beautiful (1998)
The Curious Case of Benjamin Button (2008)

Exercises

I. Everyone has experienced trauma in their lives. What is your own worst tragedy? How did the incident affect you? Can you build a story around that particular incident?

2.   Imagine a tragedy, such as the death of a loved one. Now create a character that has the most to lose because of that tragedy. Write a two-page scene in which the character discovers that the tragedy has occurred.

3.   Big blockbuster films are often accused of being heartless because they don't contain enough personal stakes. Take your least favorite blockbuster and imagine higher personal stakes for the hero. How would these stakes change the story? What would these stakes add to the characters and the storyline?

Chapter Five

KING LEAR

"More than kin and less than kind":
Want to create a classic drama? Destroy a family.

*K*ING LEAR IS A BRUTAL PLAY filled with cruelty and disasters. As Lear divides his estate among three children, the family implodes, leaving both Lear and his kingdom in ruins. By the end, Lear is a madman, naked in a storm, alone and dying. The play speaks to the pain and love unique to families, and reveals the resentment and violence that underlies the closest ties. It is an epic story of abomination and transcendence, a timeless classic in every sense.

There's a good reason why classics like *King Lear* so often focus on family. The family unit has been with us since the dawn of time. Our fundamental human need for family is both primal and painfully complex — which is exactly why it makes for such good drama.

Of course, not all family dramas are created equal. What makes for a classic? What can we learn from *King Lear*?

START AT THE ROOT

All writers search for an opening sequence, hoping to make it pop. The opening sequence for a family drama must reveal the source of this particular family's conflict and set the stage for every fight the family will have. Every family drama must start at the root.

The first scene of King Lear begins with a test designed by Lear to determine which child loves him the most. All his kids have to do is profess their devotion. Easy, right? Wrong.

Regan and Goneril, the older sisters, speak first. They go and on, trying to outdo each other with their beautifully con responses. Cordelia, the youngest, is disgusted by their panderi as she resolves to "love, and be silent," Lear turns to her:

LEAR: *What can you say to draw a third more opulent than your sisters?*
Speak.
CORDELIA: *Nothing, my lord.*
LEAR: *Nothing?*
CORDELIA: *Nothing.*
LEAR: *Nothing will come of nothing: speak again.*
CORDELIA: *Unhappy that I am, I cannot heave*
My heart into my mouth. I love your majesty
According to my bond; no more nor less. (Act I, scene I)

Cordelia knows what's expected of her but she refuses to play the game. She is bent on telling the truth — in striking contrast to her sisters, who are willing to say whatever is necessary to get what they want. Furious, Lear banishes the one daughter who actually loves him.

The opening scene exposes the root of the family problem: Lear doesn't know his own children. His ignorance is the source of the whole tragedy. The play ends with Lear finally figuring out who his children are — just as he's about to die.

The opening sequence of the movie *Extremely Loud & Incredibly Close* (2011) sets up the family dynamic beautifully. It begins with a flashback, in which Oskar (Thomas Horn) eagerly follows his beloved father (Tom Hanks) on a quest to find the "Lost Sixth Burrough" of New York City. Through the whole sequence, Oskar's mother (Sandra Bullock) is marginalized; she is always there, but she seems remote and indifferent, like she's too self-absorbed to pay attention to her son. When we flash forward in the action, we learn that Oskar's father has been killed in the 9/11 attack, and that Oskar is still unable to connect with his mother. By the end of the story, Oskar discovers that his mother was always watching him, every step of the way, spending hours quietly following his every movement. The tender moment allows Oskar and his mother to find a way to get past the tragedy and love each other. The moment wouldn't have its power if it hadn't been set up in those crucial first scenes.

THE POINT OF NO RETURN

We begin *King Lear* believing that it is a tragedy about Lear's incapacity to understand his children. But in one exquisitely painful scene, everything we understand about this play gets completely reversed. It is the point of no return for Lear and his family — nothing can ever be the same again.

The scene begins with Lear leaving his daughter Goneril's house. He is angry that Goneril put half his men out of her house, claiming she doesn't have space to keep them. Lear appeals to his other daughter, Regan, assuming that she will take him and his men in. But that's not at all what happens. To his surprise, Regan sides with Goneril:

> GONERIL: *What need you five and twenty, ten, or five,*
> *To follow in a house where twice so many*
> *Have a command to tend you?*
> REGAN: *What need one?*
> LEAR: *O, reason not the need!* (Act 2, scene 4)

Regan and Goneril gang up on their father like a two-headed shark: one starts a thought, the other finishes it, and at the end Lear ends up with nothing. His plaintive "O, reason not the need!" is his final plea to their better natures. Without the power to command, who is Lear? How can he be the king, or even a father, if no one even listens to his requests? It is the moment Lear knows he is cornered. He knows that Regan and Goneril are working together against him. And he knows they will win.

The scene reveals a stunning reversal of power: it's now the daughters who have the authority to banish. Instead of using that power wisely, they torture their father. The audience's understanding of the tragedy shifts as a result: Lear may not know his children, but no parent deserves this.

The point of no return is a common feature of basic script structure. It usually occurs at the midpoint of the script and features a reversal of fortune or major revelation. In family dramas, that moment is marked by a dramatic change in the family dynamic. In the classic *Shadow of a Doubt* (1943), for instance, that change occurs when young Charlie (Teresa Wright) accuses her uncle (Joseph Cotten) of being a murderer. She wants him to leave town to avoid a horrible scandal for the family; he refuses to go. At the tipping point, Charlie wears the emerald ring her uncle gave her — the one that can prove he's guilty — to dinner. Charlie's threat is blatantly clear, and the balance of power shifts immediately. What Charlie doesn't realize is that her brazen defiance may cost her her life. The moment she wears that ring is the point of no return, and it spells doom.

CATHARSIS

Catharsis is not easy to define. Simply put, it is a term used to describe an emotional outpouring at the end of a story. In cathartic moments, the outpouring of emotion leads to closure for both the characters and the audience. According to Aristotle, no drama is complete without it.

The catharsis in *King Lear* comes in the very last lines. Having been thrown out into the stormy night by Regan and Goneril, Lear goes mad. Naked and cold, he discovers that the one daughter who always loved him, Cordelia, is dead. Lear is stunned. He howls at the heavens, ranting wildly, calling out his despairing question: "Why should a dog, a horse, a rat, have life, / And thou no breath at all?" Lear sinks down, gently cradling her as he laments:

> *Thou'lt come no more,*
> *Never, never, never, never, never!* (Act 5, scene 3)

Lear says the word "never" over and over again, as if he is trying to convince himself to face the truth. The repetition echoes the sound of Lear's heart breaking. In that moment, Lear realizes that all is lost and gone — and that it was his fault. The weight of the realization is crushing. He dies suddenly, with the truth on his lips.

The cathartic scene is a fundamental to the story. It allows Lear a moment to recognize what has happened and why. He has needlessly destroyed his kingdom, realm, and family. The recognition of his mistake heightens the tragedy, because his one moment of true clarity is also the moment of his death.

Perhaps the best family drama ever filmed, *The Godfather* (1972) trilogy begins with Michael (Al Pacino), a decorated war hero and a college boy, bringing his girlfriend Kay to his sister's wedding. When she asks how they know the famous wedding singer, Johnny Fontaine, he tells her the story of how his father strong-armed Fontaine's bandleader with an offer he couldn't refuse. Kay is horrified, but Michael replies: "That's my family, Kay, not me." Though Michael initially denies that he will become involved in the family business, at the midpoint Michael volunteers to murder two men to avenge his father. By the end of the first movie, he has transformed into a ruthless killer. In *The Godfather: Part II* (1974) Michael sinks to a new low, murdering his own brother Fredo. He has become everything that he rejected at the beginning of the first movie.

The Godfather, © 1972 Paramount, All Rights Reserved.

The catharsis occurs in the last moments of *The Godfather: Part III* (1990). Wracked with guilt over the death of Fredo, Michael attempts to leave the Mafia. He wants a normal life, free of violence, for himself and also for his family. His chief concern is protecting his children, and particularly his daughter Mary. But it is already too late for Michael: "Just when I thought I was out," he says, "they pull me back in." Michael goes in for one final deal. In the final moments of the movie, the deal goes awry. As Michael takes Mary to the opera house to see her brother, Anthony, perform, assassins infiltrate the gallery. Bullets fly. Michael is wounded. He tries to protect his daughter, but she's hit. Mary dies in his arms as Michael screams in agony.

The movie ends with Michael seated alone in the back yard of Don Tommasino's Sicilian villa. He is an old man. A montage of all the loved ones he has lost flashes before his eyes: Mary, Kay, and his first wife, Apollonia. His life of crime and violence has destroyed everything that he has ever truly loved. As Michael contemplates his guilt, he slumps over and dies alone. As with Lear, clarity comes for Michael only in the moments before death. It is that final cathartic realization that brings the emotional closure for both Michael and the audience.

Every classic family drama has a moment of catharsis at the end. It may or may not come with absolution, but it always happens. Giving your characters a moment for closure allows both the characters and the audience to take in the full scope of what has happened in the story.

Classic dramas cling to everlasting themes of love and family because they matter to audiences. They show us joy and pain, and then give us the closure that so many of us search for all our lives.

KEY POINTS TO REMEMBER

† The opening sequence must reveal the source of this particular family's conflict and set the stage for every fight the family will have.

† After the midpoint, give us a "point of no return": a dramatic change or reversal in the family dynamic.

✝ At the end, make sure to give your characters and your audience a cathartic moment.

✝ Make sure your cathartic moment has an outpouring of emotion that leads to closure for both the characters and the audience.

Movies to Watch

Shadow of a Doubt (1943)
The Godfather (1972); *The Godfather: Part II* (1974);
The Godfather: Part III (1990)
Extremely Loud & Incredibly Close (2011)

Exercises

1. Write a two-page scene based on the biggest family fight you ever experienced or witnessed, and then embellish it to make it ten times worse.

2. Imagine a family skeleton — something painful or terrible. Then create two characters: one trying to expose the secret, and one trying to hide it. Generate an outline for their story. Will the skeleton be exposed or remain hidden? Will it destroy the family?

3. Not all families are traditional nuclear families. Think of an alternate version of family, and then follow the steps for Exercise 2. What is the skeleton in their closet? Who is trying to expose the secret, and who is trying to hide it? What is at stake for each character?

Chapter Six

A Midsummer Night's Dream

"As luck would have it":
A good comedy requires at least one accident,
coincidence, or ironic twist.

A MIDSUMMER NIGHT'S DREAM IS A FARCICAL COLLECTION of accidents, coincidences, and ironic twists. Unlike any other play in Shakespeare's canon, *A Midsummer Night's Dream* is completely divorced from reality.

Far from being put off by all the absurdities, audiences love this play. Of all Shakespeare's plays, it is the most frequently performed. Always on the docket for prominent troupes like The Royal Shakespeare Company, the play is a perennial crowd-pleaser.

How, exactly, do accidents, coincidences, and twists of fate function in this play? Why are they so useful? And how can we translate their charm to the big screen?

ACCIDENTS

Accidents happen every day. We've all experienced one — a dropped phone, a slip-and-fall, a fender bender. But accidents in stories are very different. They set the plot in motion and define the course of the narrative. In stories, the true pleasure of accidents is not the accident itself but rather how it affects everyone and everything in the story, or what's known as the "ripple effect." If you put an accident into your story, the audience needs to see exactly how that accident affects both the characters and the plot.

A Midsummer Night's Dream begins with a complex love triangle. Two men, Demetrius and Lysander, are in love with Hermia. Hermia loves Lysander. Hermia's best friend, Helena, is in love with Deme-trius. Confused yet? Just wait: it gets more complicated. Hermia and Lysander take off into the forest on their way to elope. Demetrius follows, hoping to stop them. Then Helena follows Demetrius. Enter Puck, a fairy in the service of Oberon, the king of the fairies. Puck decides to right the triangle by placing a love potion into their eyes. When they wake, he says, they will all be in love with the right person. But this is not what happens. When they all wake, both men are now in love with Helena, Hermia's best friend.

By simple accident, the wrong potion gets into the wrong eyes. Of course, Oberon immediately scolds Puck ("What hast thou done?") and insists that Puck remedy his mistake. The characters spend the rest of the time in the forest chasing one another around like madmen, with Puck fruitlessly attempting to intervene. Some of the funniest scenes in the play occur in this section of text. But the delight of those scenes is not about the accident proper, but rather about the effects of that accident. As we watch it ripple outward in one scene after the next, each character is given a chance to react, and each reaction is funnier than the last.

Being There (1979) is built around this ripple effect. In the first act of the film, Chance (Peter Sellers), a simple-minded gardener, acci-dentally steps into the street and gets hit by a limousine. In that limo is Eve Rand, the wife of the man who happens to be a good friend of the U.S. President. One thing leads to another, and Chance ends up offering common gardening advice to the President ("growth has it seasons") only to have that advice misinterpreted as shrewd political commentary ("I think what our insightful young friend is saying is that we welcome the inevitable seasons of nature, but we're upset by the seasons of our economy"). By the end of the movie, Chance is the heir to Rand's estate and the favorite to replace the President in the next election cycle. One accident turns someone with "rice pudding between his ears" into the most powerful man in the world — and it is hilarious.

COINCIDENCES

Many writers believe that coincidences are a cheat. When done well, however, a coincidence can do something remarkable. It can remind the audience that life is unpredictable — in both wonderful and terrible ways. What accounts for the difference between a well-done coincidence and a cheat is simple: a cheat is an easy answer to a narrative problem; a well-done coincidence advances the plot.

A Midsummer Night's Dream presents one coincidence after the next. For instance, it is entirely a coincidence that Puck is walking through the forest carrying a love potion when he stumbles on the four lovers. It's also a coincidence that Oberon and Titania, king and queen of the fairies, are locked in a battle for power on the same exact night that the four lovers wander into the forest. The two battles — one for love, the other for power — just happen to occur in the exact same area of the forest. But that's not enough for Shakespeare. There also happens to be a cluster of muddle-minded actors working on their play. Rather than acting as quick narrative fixes, each one of these coincidences becomes central to the plot. Could we imagine this play without Titania falling in love with Bottom? All three groups — the lovers, the actors, and the fairies — end up inextricably intertwined, all over the course of one fateful night.

When Harry Met Sally... (1989) is littered with coincidences. Every time Harry meets Sally is a coincidence. The story begins when Harry (Billy Crystal) needs a ride to New York City, and Sally (Meg Ryan) happens to be going the same way. Harry and Sally part ways in New York City, only to meet again five years later when they both happen to be boarding the same airplane. Again they part ways, and again they bump into each other five years later — only this time, they become friends. Interspersed in the movie are documentary-style interviews with elderly couples telling stories of how they met: a couple who were born on the same day and in the same hospital; a couple who were separated after high school ran into each other on the street years later; a couple who got divorced and then remarried after they bumped into each other at a funeral. Coincidence is not only central to the plot, it becomes a unique theme in this movie: love is a fluke, the movie tells us, which is part of what makes love so special.

IRONIC TWIST

Every good comedy has an ironic twist. An ironic twist takes the events of the story and gives it deeper meaning both for the characters and the audience, providing a lesson. Like accidents and coincidences, ironic twists must be integral to the plot.

In the first scene of *A Midsummer Night's Dream*, Hermia's father Egeus drags his daughter in front of Theseus, the ruler of Athens. Egeus wants Hermia to marry Demetrius, but Hermia wants to marry Lysander. Of course, Demetrius is in love with Hermia, which only strengthens her father's case. But the real issue is that the laws of Athens dictate that her father has the right to order Hermia's death if she doesn't marry whomever her father wishes. It is certainly a strange way to start a comedy. What kind of law would give a father such power? What kind of father would decide to use it?

The set-up for the ironic twist occurs in the forest. Like all the others, Demetrius is given the love potion. But unlike all the others, Demetrius is never freed from its effects — he is the only one still drugged at the end of the play. Ironically, the man who started all the trouble is left madly in love with one person he dislikes. The chaotic night in the forest, with all its unpredictable accidents and coincidences, has a lasting impact. In the final sequence, Egeus allows Hermia to marry Lysander, and Theseus abolishes the antiquated rule. With Demetrius' magical change of heart, all that was wrong at the beginning of the play is now right.

Wedding Crashers (2005) is loaded with ironic twists. At the plot's start, John (Owen Wilson) and Jeremy (Vince Vaughn) have clear prohibitions against falling in love. Acting as each other's wingman, they go to weddings, eat, drink, and find women to have sex with — but they are never, ever supposed to fall in love with them. This, of course, is exactly what happens. At the Cleary wedding, John falls head-over-heels for Claire and Jeremy embarks on a twisted romance with her sister, Gloria. In the last scene, John crashes Jeremy's wedding to Gloria, only this time, it's not to find women to have sex with, it's because John truly loves one of the guests: Claire. The scene is the exact opposite of how the movie started, complete with John admitting it was wrong to deceive Claire. Ironically, that deception actually ends up leading everyone to the truth: John finds true love; Jeremy finds his true equal; and Claire discovers her true feelings for her boyfriend Sack. The last image is of the four — John, Jeremy, Claire, and Gloria — driving off into the sunset to crash a wedding together.

Wedding Crashers, © 2005 New Line, All Rights Reserved.

KEY POINTS TO REMEMBER

† Accidents should set the plot in motion and define the course of the narrative.

† The true pleasure of accidents is not the accident itself but rather how it affects everyone and everything in the story, or what's known as the *ripple effect.*

† Well-done coincidences can remind the audience that life is unpredictable — in both wonderful and terrible ways.

† A cheat is an easy answer to a narrative problem; a well-done coincidence advances the plot.

† An ironic twist takes the events of the story and gives it deeper meaning both for the characters and the audience, providing a lesson learned at the end of the story.

† Like accidents and coincidences, ironic twists must be integral to the plot.

MOVIES TO WATCH

Being There (1979)
When Harry Met Sally... (1989)
Wedding Crashers (2005)

EXERCISES

1. Think of an accident that has happened in your own life. Now imagine a chain of events that would radically change your life (in either positive or negative ways) because of that accident. Write a quick one-page outline for the story, tracking the ripple effect. Where would the accident lead you?

2. Set up a story for an unlikely pair that must work together to win, say, a pie-eating contest. Imagine an accident or coincidence that brought them together. Where and how did they meet? Are they friends or enemies? What happens at the end of their story?

3. Think of your favorite comedy. Does it contain an accident, coincidence, or ironic twist? If so, what makes that accident, coincidence, or ironic twist appealing to you?

Chapter Seven

THE TAMING OF THE SHREW

"The course of true love never did run smooth":
Or, nobody wants to watch a happy couple.

*T*HE *TAMING OF THE SHREW* IS NOT what most people think of as a traditional romance. Far from the lovely lyrical lines of *Romeo and Juliet*, this play tells the unromantic story of a how Petruchio, a pig-headed hick, subdues Kate, a stubborn hothead. Yet, the play has become a template for popular romances in Western culture, including romantic comedies. Why?

The play stages one of the oldest battles on the books: the war of the sexes. It's a war that is still going on today, and probably will forever. It's a universal theme that taps into our primal need for sex and power, two of Hollywood's favorite subjects.

What makes the battle between Kate and Petruchio sizzle? What makes it romantic? How can we capture that passion in our own scripts?

FRICTION

If you're going to stage a battle of the sexes, you have to start with the conflict, and the conflict should always come from character. Giving the characters diametrically opposing views creates friction — the main ingredient for romantic sparks.

No two characters could be more opposed than Kate and Petruchio. She is curt, spiteful, and sharp-tongued. He is arrogant, rough, and rude. From the minute they first meet, the two engage in verbal warfare, trading barbs and foul insults. Sound like a recipe for romance? Not really. Yet, the scene absolutely crackles with energy:

KATE: *If I be waspish, best beware my sting.*
PETRUCHIO: *My remedy is then to pluck it out.*
KATE: *Ay, if the fool could find it where it lies.*
PETRUCHIO: *Who knows not where a wasp does wear his sting? In his tail.*
KATE: *In his tongue.*
PETRUCHIO: *Whose tongue?*
KATE: *Yours, if you talk of tails: and so farewell.*
PETRUCHIO: *What, my tongue in your tail? Nay, come again, Good Kate; I am a gentleman.*
KATE: *That I'll try.*
   (She strikes him.) (Act 2, scene 1)

What starts as a conversation about Kate's "tail" ends up in not-so-subtle sexual innuendo, the scene racing forward with quick, short lines and ending in an explosion of physical force — mimicking the pattern of sexual friction and release. Their chemistry is obvious even as they tear each other apart with words.

The scene titillates in every way possible. Just as importantly, it sets the two characters at odds. Keeping them at odds in the beginning gives the story somewhere to go by the end — and with romances, we all know they will end up together.

The Empire Strikes Back (1980) isn't technically a romantic comedy, but it does include one of the most celebrated romances on film: that of Princess Leia and Han Solo. Like *The Taming of the Shrew*, the dialogue contains vibrant banter laden with sexual energy. In one of their most famous exchanges, Han (Harrison Ford) accuses Leia (Carrie Fisher) of having the hots for him when she asks him to stay. Of course, she denies it:

LEIA: *You're imagining things.*
HAN: *Am I? Then why are you following me? Afraid I was going to leave without giving you a goodbye kiss?*
LEIA: *I'd just as soon kiss a Wookie.*
HAN: *I can arrange that. You could use a good kiss.*

The scene sizzles because we all know that Han is not imagining things — and we know they could both use a good kiss. Han does not actually end up kissing Leia here, but in the next sequence, their action lines demand bodily contact:

> (*The ship jolts unexpectedly. Leia stumbles into Han Solo's arms.*)
> LEIA: *Let go, please.*
> HAN: *(listening) Shh!*
> LEIA: *Let go!*
> HAN: *Don't get excited.*
> LEIA: *Captain, being held by you isn't quite enough to get me excited.*
> HAN: *Sorry sweetheart. We don't have time for anything else.*

Like the exchanges between Kate and Petruchio, Han and Leia's repartee features short, quick lines and double entendres. The magic of their scenes together lies in the mind/body split: intense physical connection versus verbal warfare. The intoxicating combination generates friction — and sexual chemistry — that buzzes with energy.

The Empire Strikes Back, © 1980 20th Century Fox, All Rights Reserved.

FUN & GAMES

In the second part a romance, we get the fun and games. While neither of the characters have committed to love, at least not consciously, they begin to play together in ways that lovers do.

For Kate and Petruchio, the fun and games start in Act 4. On their way home to Kate's father's house, Petruchio engages her in a verbal match. He argues that that the sun is actually the moon. Kate catches on quickly, but just as she agrees it is the moon, he says it is the sun again. If the servant attending them is confused, the old man who enters their game in the middle is more confused. Petruchio asks Kate: "Hast thou beheld a fresher gentlewoman?" Kate responds in agreement by calling the old man a "young budding virgin, fair and fresh." Together they taunt the old man in a way that recalls the play of language in their first meeting, only this time the banter is sweet and fun.

Watching the characters play together is essential to building a romance. *The Artist* (2011), for instance, begins with actor George Valentin (Jean Dujardin) meeting a young ingénue, Peppy Miller (Bérénice Bejo), at the premiere of his latest movie. The next day, George and Peppy run into each other again on the set, only they don't know it. George sees two lovely legs dancing from behind a lowered screen; he begins to dance, too, and then they dance together in perfect harmony without even seeing each other's faces. When the screen lifts, a look of recognition passes between them: they are meant for each other. It is a delightful moment, and one that sets us up perfectly the romance between the two characters. George and Peppy get together at the end of the movie, but the romance needed the middle step of fun and games to allow their affections to develop. Without it, the audience wouldn't believe that they are truly in love.

The Artist, © 2011 Sony, All Rights Reserved.

RESOLUTION

The end-goal of every romance is to bring the two characters together. Whether it's suggested or explicitly shown, the audience needs to see the moment when the two characters unite.

In *The Taming of the Shrew*, it is in the final lines of the play that Kate and Petruchio truly come together. To prove that Kate has changed, Petruchio proposes a wager to the other bridegrooms. The three will send for their wives, and whoever's wife answers first will win the bet. Of course, everyone believes the first to answer will be mild-mannered Bianca, but it is Kate who comes the moment Petruchio calls. Added to that, Kate launches into a long speech about the nature of love and obedience. It is both a measure of her obedience and a token of her affection. At the end, Petruchio catches her up in his arms and utters the most famous lines of the play: "Come on and kiss me, Kate!" Their verbal jousting finished, Petruchio takes her hand and leads her to bed.

Kisses are one of the most common resolutions for a romance. The madcap final sequence of *Bringing Up Baby* (1938) features Susan (Katharine Hepburn) scaling a ladder next to the giant Brontosaurus skeleton that David (Cary Grant) has painstakingly put together. Perched on the ladder, she peppers him with questions, attempting to extract a confession of love — just before she topples over, taking the whole Brontosaurus skeleton with her. The last lines point to resolution without saying it directly:

> SUSAN: *Oh, David, can you ever forgive me?*
> DAVID: *I... I... I...*
> SUSAN: *You can! And you still love me.*
> DAVID: *Susan, that... that...*
> SUSAN: *You do. Oh, David.*
> DAVID: *Oh, dear. Oh, my.*

They fall into each other's arms and kiss. The audience knows that he loves her, even if he never explicitly states it. No matter how it happens, the conclusion of a romance must provide the crucial resolution that the audience longs for. The job of the writer is to first create that romantic longing, and then fulfill it — in whatever way works best for the story.

KEY POINTS TO REMEMBER

† Giving the two characters diametrically opposed views creates friction — the main ingredient for romantic sparks.

† Romances needs a middle step of fun and games to allow affections to develop; without it, the audience won't believe that they are truly in love.

† Make sure your romance has a fulfilling resolution, whether it be a hope, a kiss, or a promise.

MOVIES TO WATCH

Bringing Up Baby (1938)
The Empire Strikes Back (1980)
The Artist (2011)

EXERCISES

1. Anyone who has been in romantic relationship has "deal-breakers." They are the things you couldn't possibly stand in another person. Or... could you? Write down your own biggest deal-breaker. Then create a character around that deal-breaker — someone who is your polar opposite. What would that character be like? What kind of friction would it cause? Can you imagine a scenario that would generate romantic sparks?

2. Write a quick two-page scene between you and this character in which you meet for the first time — and your imaginary character is doing the thing that bugs you the most. Where are you? What are you doing? How does the scene begin? How does it end?

3. Think of your favorite romantic comedy. Who are the two lead characters? What are their individual traits, and how are they diametrically opposed? What makes the movie romantic, in your opinion?

Chapter Eight

HENRY V

"Some have greatness thrust upon 'em":
Flawed heroes are the only ones worth caring about.

*H*ENRY V IS SHAKESPEARE'S MOST STRIKING PORTRAIT OF A HERO. It tells the story of a young king who leads a ragtag band of Englishmen to victory over an enormous French army. He is inspiring, brave, and victorious. But what's interesting about the story is that he is also deeply flawed. Far from putting the audience off, Henry's flaws engage our sympathy.

Every hero needs a flaw. Watching the hero suffer under the weight of his flaws allows the audience to see themselves in the character. Just as importantly, flaws add to the drama. It gives the character something to prove. When the hero finally overcomes his flaws at the plot's climax, the audience cheers — not only because they see themselves in the hero, but also because the hero worked so hard to do it.

What are Henry V's flaws? How does he overcome them? How can we create a heroic character like this in our own stories?

HAUNTED BY THE PAST

Henry V begins as a king with a sordid past. While his father ruthlessly deposed and killed Richard II to take the throne, the young Henry spent his time drinking and whoring in dirty, low-class pubs. His best friends were thieves, robbers, and drunks — and those were the nice ones. Asked if Henry will make a good and faithful king, the Archbishop of Canterbury replies, "The course of his youth promised it not." Henry V is an immature, reckless fool. He is no one's idea of a good monarch.

Or so everyone believes at the beginning of the play. By the end we know that he was one of the greatest kings England ever had. What changes? And why start this way?

Giving your hero a sordid past allows you to show change. The hero begins the story haunted by his own history; by the end, he faces down his past and demonstrates his growth. It is a simple — but powerful — formula.

The moment to face the past comes for Henry V near the end of Act 3. On the march to Agincourt — the plot's big battle scene — Henry is pulled aside by one of his officers, Pistol. Henry's old friend from the pub, Bardolph, has been caught stealing from a church. Pistol implores Henry to give special consideration to Bardolph — he is Henry's good friend, whom Henry has loved since he was a child. But as the king, Henry can offer no such leniency. Despite the tears running down his face, Henry sentences Bardolph to death for his crime. Gone are Henry's foolish childhood affections; in its place is the mature and righteous justice of a king.

Like Henry V, Tony Stark in *Iron Man* (2008) is a man with a past. At the beginning of the movie, Tony (Robert Downey, Jr.) is a drunk and a womanizer. The CEO of Stark Industries, Tony manufactures dangerous weapons without any concern for how they get used. In the opening sequence, we watch him sip bourbon as he nonchalantly unleashes the monstrous killing machine called Jericho. He is everything that's wrong with the Military Industrial Complex. But all this changes when Tony gets kidnapped. Ironically, he is wounded in the attack by his own weapons. In the end, Tony takes responsibility for the dangers his weapons present, and in the final sequence he destroys his own weapons factory. His past goes up in a fiery blaze as he becomes a hero.

FESTERING WOUNDS

Giving your protagonist a wound — either physical or mental — handicaps them against the competition, making the challenges they face just that much more daunting. Before they can truly become a hero, they must find a way to close the wound.

Henry V receives his wound in the first few scenes of the play. Gathering his counselors, he contemplates war with France over land rights. In response to Henry's claim, the French Dauphin sends him a "treasure." When Henry opens it, he discovers neither gold nor gems, but tennis balls. Attached is a snide note saying that games are "meeter for [his] spirit" than war. The French know of Henry's sordid past, of course, and they have no intention of taking his threats seriously. The taunt is cruel — its words are meant to wound not only Henry, but all of England. It must be righted, and Henry means to do so with blood and bone.

And that he does. Proving that he is no foolish boy, Henry and his scrappy band of three hundred followers kill ten thousand Frenchmen at Agincourt while losing only twenty-five Englishmen in the process. The bloody massacre leaves the French no choice but to acknowledge Henry V as a force to be reckoned with. Just as importantly, they have to take back the wounding words spoken at the beginning of the play. In his final lines, the Dauphin opines:

> *All is confounded, all!*
> *Reproach and everlasting shame*
> *Sits mocking in our plumes.* (Act 4, scene 5)

The Dauphin mocked Henry with tennis balls; now "everlasting shame" mocks him. The score has been settled, and with it, Henry V has become a legend.

Like Henry V, Maverick in *Top Gun* (1986) has a reputation for reckless, wild behavior. And like Henry V, Maverick (Tom Cruise) is a wounded hero. Throughout the movie, we hear over and over again that Maverick is haunted by the loss of his father. "Is that why you fly the way you do?," Viper asks Maverick, "Trying to prove something?" But things only get worse. At the lowpoint, Maverick loses control of his plane and goes down, killing his best friend Goose in the process. At the climax of the film, Maverick's plane is called to a real dog-fight. Struggling with the shadow of his father and the pain of losing Goose, Maverick must find a way to overcome his fears. The sequence ends with Maverick tossing Goose's dog tags into the ocean — proof that he has found a way to close the wound and become a true hero.

Top Gun, © 1986 Paramount, All Rights Reserved.

UNTESTED AND UNTRIED

Not only is Henry V a king with a sordid past, he has no experience running a kingdom or making decisions to invade other countries. He's never even been to a war — let alone won one. He is the essence of the untested and untried hero.

Having an untested and untried hero does two remarkable things for a character. First, it makes the final challenge more difficult. Second, it gives the hero something to prove. Both elements must come together at the climax, when the hero finally succeeds.

And Henry V certainly succeeds. At the climax, Henry and his three hundred tired, hungry English fighters face an enormous garrison of well-trained, well-fed Frenchmen. The French have every advantage, but Henry does not give up. In answer to his cousin Westermerland's wish that they had more men, Henry gives his most famous speech:

> *If we are mark'd to die, we are enough*
> *To do our country loss; and if to live,*
> *The fewer men, the greater share of honor.*
> *...This story shall the good man teach his son;*
> *And Crispin Crispian shall ne'er go by,*
> *From this day to the ending of the world,*
> *But we in it shall be remember'd;*
> *We few, we happy few, we band of brothers;*
> *For he today that sheds his blood with me*
> *Shall be my brother; be he ne'er so vile,*
> *This day shall gentle his condition;*
> *And gentlemen in England now a-bed*
> *Shall think themselves accursed they were not here,*
> *And hold their manhoods cheap while any speaks*
> *That fought with us upon Saint Crispin's day.* (Act 4, scene 3)

The lines are designed to send chills down the spine. Rather than seeing their paltry numbers as a disadvantage, Henry turns it into an opportunity: "the fewer men, the greater share of honor." He is *happy* there are so few. It is an unexpected — and genius — turn of rhetoric.

Of course, Henry V proves to be more than just rhetoric. Henry and his Englishmen fight their hearts out and win. In doing so, Henry proves himself as not only a good warrior and a good leader, but also as a hero capable of overcoming his wounds and jettisoning his past. He becomes the tried and tested embodiment of true and faithful kingship — and one of the greatest that England has ever known.

The character of Clarice Starling in *The Silence of the Lambs* (1991) is both untested and untried at the beginning of the story. The movie opens with Clarice (Jodie Foster) as a young student at the FBI Academy. She's never been in the field, let alone solved a case. When she begins work on the Buffalo Bill serial murder case, she's not even a full-fledged agent yet. Through the course of the movie, Clarice gets a crash course in criminal psychology from one of the most heinous villains ever portrayed on screen: Hannibal Lecter. By the end, she proves that she can stand up to Lecter, solve a case, save the victim, and then take down a killer — alone, and in a dark house. We end where we began: the final scene is at the FBI Academy, only this time, it's her graduation.

Like Henry V, Clarice overcomes her inexperience and naiveté. By the end of the movie, she has more than earned her stripes as one of the most remarkable heroes committed to film.

Key Points to Remember

† Giving your hero a flaw engages the audience's sympathy and makes the character more relatable.

† Flaws add to the drama by giving the character something to overcome.

† Giving your hero a mental wound or a sordid past allows you to show how the character grows and changes by the end.

† By the end, the hero must overcome his flaws, his wounds, and his past.

Movies to Watch

Top Gun (1986)
The Silence of the Lambs (1991)
Iron Man (2008)

Exercises

I.   Think of your favorite movie. What is the hero's strength? What is his flaw? How does that flaw play into the final climactic battle?

2.   If you are working on a script, list out the qualities of your hero. Does your hero have a flaw, a mental wound, or a sordid past? How does your hero overcome it at the end?

3. Chose a flaw and build a hypothetical character around that flaw. What does your character want? What is his flaw? How does the challenge the character faces at the end of the story force him to overcome his flaw?

Chapter Nine

JULIUS CAESAR

"An honest tale speeds best":
How history proves that creativity is overrated.

M OST WRITERS BELIEVE that creativity is the most important element in storytelling. We spend hours trying to come up with something new and fresh with a twist ending that'll surprise the audience.

But *Julius Caesar* isn't particularly creative in the traditional sense. It basically rips off a known historical event — the murder of a Roman emperor — and puts it on the stage. Yet, it's one of Shakespeare's most enduringly popular texts. Why?

Historical movies have always been tremendously popular in Hollywood. In fact, one of the highest-grossing films of all time is based on a historical event: *Titanic* (1997). Year after year, audiences flock to historical movies — proving time and again that they absolutely adore going "behind the scenes" of stories they're already familiar with.

Why do audiences love histories? What makes these stories so compelling?

TELL US SECRETS

Historical figures are celebrities from the long past. Just as audiences want to know the secrets and private lives of modern celebrities, they want to know the secrets and private lives of historical figures.

In *Julius Caesar*, the main event is Caesar's murder. But who was involved? Why did they do it? How could they betray such a great man? Shakespeare's play not only produces salacious details of how and why the conspirators plotted the murder, it also offers a recreation of the bloody death scene. In addition, the audience gets a look at Caesar's private, tender moments with his wife Calpurnia and his friend Marc Antony. It's the story behind the story that audiences are looking for — and in this play, it's exactly what audiences get.

Bonnie and Clyde (1967) tells the story of two real-life gangsters. When the film was released, it caused a sensation because of its graphic references to sex and gritty blood-soaked violence. In one scene, Clyde (Warren Beatty) places his gun between his legs while Bonnie (Faye Dunaway) strokes it — and then the scene gets dirty. In fact, the intertwining of sex and violence is so pronounced with this famous couple, and the cultural impact so wide, that psychologists actually named a disease after them: the "Bonnie and Clyde Syndrome," or *hybristophilia*, involves being sexually aroused by people who have committed a gruesome crime. The movie provides a thrilling look at the private lives of two extremely dangerous people. The audience loves it not for what they already know, but rather for what they don't: the sexy, secret, scandalous details.

GIVE US A HERO

Stories about real-life heroes are perennial crowd pleasers. Whether from modern day or the distant past, the dynamic combination of true events and heroism produces extraordinary stories, time and again.

Julius Caesar gives the audience a classic hero: Caesar is bold, humble, and wise enough to know that Cassius is not the friend he pretends to be. But we also see that he is in danger. In the first few lines of the play, the soothsayer issues her famous warning about the Ides of March. A few lines later, Cassius and his gang of schemers appear and plot the murder of Caesar. The urgent succession of events ends in Act 3 with the bloody death of Caesar. The murder is electrifying: with gruesome solemnity, one conspirator after another steps up to stab him. The episode concludes with the famous lines delivered by Caesar to his trusted advisor, Brutus: "Et tu, Brute?" ("And you, Brutus?").

While the bloody murder in Act 3 makes for a great drama, it leaves Shakespeare without a hero. Rather than ending the play there, Shakespeare gives us a new hero: Marc Antony. At the eulogy, Marc Antony delivers his famous speech ("Friends, Romans, Countrymen, lend me your ears"). His speech rouses the crowd, eventually leading to the deaths of the conspirators. Shakespeare painstakingly frames Antony as the new hero. No matter what the historical event or how it plays out, the audience expects a hero.

The audience for this play, both then and now, knows that Caesar will die before the play even starts. The key to the play's emotional success is the clear heroism of Caesar and Antony. The audience needs to be attached to Caesar in order to grieve when he is lost. Watching Antony mourn — and then rise — heightens the audience's response.

Of course, not every historical event yields an obvious hero. Even if there isn't one naturally written into the historical event, the audience always needs someone to wrap their hearts and minds around. James Cameron's *Titanic* (1997), for instance, takes an event without a clear hero and transforms it into a spellbinding story of Rose and Jack (Kate Winslet and Leonardo DiCaprio). Telling the story through the eyes of this fictional couple arouses our sympathy. Because the audience identifies with Jack and Rose, we hope against hope that they both will be saved — even though we know, from history, that few survived. Their clear heroism, in the face of tragic true events, is what generates the magic in the story.

MAKE IT EPIC

Audiences want to feel as if the historical figure they are watching had an impact. They want it to matter. Telling your story on an epic scale, with a sweeping scope and plenty of spectacle, lends your story weight and meaning.

Julius Caesar is nothing if not epic. After Caesar is murdered, crowds swarm the streets of Rome, which escalates to full-scale war. Audiences are transported from Rome to the battlefields as they watch Antony and Brutus lead their armies to victory or doom.

With the clash of swords, the enemies are defeated one after another. It is an exciting end, and one that signaled the eventual fall of the Roman Republic. Caesar's death changed the face of history. In short, it *mattered.*

Epic films have a long history of focusing on historical figures: *The Ten Commandments* (1956), *Lawrence of Arabia* (1962), *Cleopatra* (1963), *Gandhi* (1982), *Braveheart* (1995), and *Elizabeth* (1998), just to name a few. *300* (2006) features a fictionalized account of the Battle of Thermopylae, in which Leonidas (Gerard Butler) and his band of three hundred loyal Spartan soldiers are forced to defend their country against a massive Persian army. It is an epic battle, and one that turned Sparta into a land of legendary strength and courage. Like *Julius Caesar*, *300* shows how the life of one vibrant hero can make a difference and be remembered forever as a result. Both *Julius Caesar* and *300* show us that history matters — and one of the ways they do so is by making it epic.

300, © 2006 Warner Bros., All Rights Reserved.

KEY POINTS TO REMEMBER

† Audiences want the inside scoop on the secret lives of historical figures, so give it to them.

† No matter what the historical event or how it plays out, the audience needs a hero.

† Audiences want to feel like the historical event mattered, so make your story epic.

Movies to Watch

Bonnie and Clyde (1967)
Titanic (1997)
300 (2006)

Exercises

1. Think of your favorite historical movie. What made the movie compelling to you? Did the hero inspire you? Were you titillated by secret, salacious, behind-the-scenes details?

2. Choose an historical event and tell the story from the perspective of an unknown hero. What new secrets could we learn about that famous event? How would this new perspective offer us a peek into private lives and the untold story behind real-life events?

3. Check out your local newspaper. Can you find a real-life hero that might make for a good story? Would it inspire others? Could that tale be told on an epic scale?

Chapter Ten

RICHARD III

"Action is eloquence":
Or, show me, don't tell me.

WHEN PEOPLE THINK OF SHAKESPEARE, they think of mono-
logues, poetry, and high-flown language. But the truth is Shakespeare's
plays are filled with action. Wars are fought, kings decapitated, women
raped, tongues ripped out, and babies murdered. These are wild, gruesome, action-packed stories.

Few are more action-packed than *Richard III*. On his way to the
throne, Richard kills no fewer than twenty people, including his best
friend, his uncle, his brothers, his wife, a half dozen cousins, and two
sweet young princes. The play tears through murders at a sickening pace
— it's a thrill-a-minute ride for the audience.

With all its action-packed exploits, *Richard III* reminds us of the
first rule of writing: show me, don't tell me. Every writer knows this
rule, but actually integrating it into your scripts is harder than it seems.
How do you make sure that your characters are active in every single
scene? How do you make that action powerful and memorable? How
can we integrate the lessons learned from this play into our scripts?

SHOW US THE GOAL

Every character has to want something. This is their "goal." At
some point in your script, each character has to reveal their goal. But
rather than having your characters *tell* us their goals, use decisive actions
to *show* it.

Richard knows exactly what he wants: to be king of England.
Every move he makes is calculated to get him closer to this goal. But
Richard doesn't waste time sitting around talking about his goals. He
doesn't threaten and he doesn't ask. Instead, he takes decisive action to

get what he needs. If he says he's going to murder his uncle, then the uncle will die in the next scene. The most heinous act Richard III is remembered for — murdering two young princes and burying their bodies under the stairs in the Tower of London — is committed with a single, chilling line: "I wish the bastards dead; and I would have it suddenly perform'd." Richard doesn't have to *tell* us how serious he is about reaching his goal; every action he takes *shows* us.

The character of Alonzo (Denzel Washington) reveals his goal at the decisive turning point of *Training Day* (2001). With his naïve trainee Jake (Ethan Hawke) in tow, Alonzo pays a visit to a drug dealer. Rather than arresting the dealer, Alonzo seizes several million dollars from underneath the floor of the dealer's kitchen, then shoots the dealer and arranges the scene to make it look like a justified shooting. At no point does Alonzo launch into a lengthy, introspective monologue on the nature of his goals. The reveal is pure action — and it's terrifying.

LESS ACTIVITY, MORE ACTION

One of the greatest temptations for writers is to add *activity*, rather than *true action*, to their scenes. "Activity" is busywork given to characters. Characters can sip a drink, shuffle papers, or nibble at food. These minor activities keep the actor busy while they're delivering their lines, but the activity involved has little or no impact on the plot or their character. "True action," by contrast, is an action that is integral to the plot and works to define your characters in a unique and interesting way.

For example, let's look at the famous fake orgasm scene in *When Harry Met Sally…* (1989). The scene starts with Harry and Sally (Billy Crystal and Meg Ryan) sitting at a restaurant arguing about fake orgasms. While they're arguing, Sally fusses with her sandwich. This is the activity in the scene. But the *true action* starts when Sally loudly — and quite convincingly — pretends to have an orgasm. The action defines Sally's relationship with Harry in a unique and interesting way: these two characters overshare intimate secrets.

The scene pops because it showcases true action. What's more, in the final moments, it manages to draw the busywork activity of eating into the final line of dialogue when the woman sitting next to Sally says to the waitress, "I'll have what she's having." The zinger weaves together both elements of action and integrates them into the fabric of the scene.

When Harry Met Sally..., © 1989 MGM, All Rights Reserved.

Shakespeare's work famously includes few stage directions. Characters enter and exit, but rarely does Shakespeare stop to tell us more than that. As a result, Shakespeare's scenes contain almost no busywork activity. The characters never sip drinks, shuffle papers, or grab coats. In fact, the only time Shakespeare adds a line of stage directions is when there is a piece of true action the audience absolutely must know in order to understand the plot.

This is certainly true in *Richard III.* In one scene after the next, Richard is either in the process of killing someone, or he's just about to. Not a single thought or movement is wasted in these scenes: every action leads directly to the accomplishment of Richard's one goal of taking over the throne of England. When Richard betrays his cousin Hastings with the words "off with his head!," the next line of stage direction we get is: "Enter Lovel and Ratcliff with Hastings' head." Absolutely none of the stage directions include superfluous activity — it's all true action. The result is a story that bristles with dramatic energy.

DUKE IT OUT

At the end of every story, the audience expects a climax. The best climaxes are riveting, exhilarating, and above all, *active*. This doesn't mean that every good climax involves the clash of sword and bone, but letting your characters duke it out — in whatever way is right for them — keeps your climaxes taut with dramatic conflict.

The final scene of *Richard III* is the epitome of a thrilling climax. Richard is surrounded by enemies. Though he knows thousands of soldiers will die, he demands the last true measure of devotion as he leads the charge. His crazed fury reaches a fever pitch as he devolves from battling for power to battling for his life. Bloodied and bruised, and about to die, he screams out: "A horse! A horse! My kingdom for a horse!" The ending sequence grips us with non-stop action from start to finish. When Richard is defeated, it is in combat, not with words. Shakespeare doesn't tell us about Richard's demise; he lets us watch it unfold in all its gruesome glory.

In the thrilling final scene of *The Departed* (2006), Staff Sgt. Dignam (Mark Wahlberg) materializes in the apartment of bad guy Colin Sullivan (Matt Damon). There's no long, drawn-out dinner conversation about why Colin did it or how Dignam is going to make him pay. Colin says only one word — "okay" — before Dignam shoots him in the head with a silencer. Yet, the scene is incredibly satisfying because we saw the climactic finale. The audience doesn't need to hear talking around the action; the action is all that is necessary — proving, yet again, the first rule of writing: *show* me, don't *tell* me.

KEY POINTS TO REMEMBER

† Rather than having your characters tell us their goals, use decisive actions to show it.

† Add true action, rather than activity, to your scenes.

† "Activity" is busywork given to characters; "true action" is integral to the plot and works to define your characters in a unique and interesting way.

† The best climaxes are riveting, exhilarating, and above all, active.

† Audiences don't need to hear a lot of talking around the action at the climax; action is all that is necessary.

MOVIES TO WATCH

When Harry Met Sally... (1989)
Training Day (2001)
The Departed (2006)

EXERCISES

1. Pick a scene from one of your scripts in which your character articulates his or her goal. For yourself, re-write the scene without any dialogue at all — just action. Make sure the actions involved demonstrate how badly that character wants to achieve his or her goal.

2. Think of an action — something radical or unique. Now take that action and build a scene around it. How does this action define the character performing it? How does it define the character's relationship with the people around them? Write up a two-page scene.

3. Go to a mall or other busy place and watch people. What insights can you gather from the actions people take? Write down your favorite moments in a file so you can use them in your writing later.

Chapter Eleven

THE WINTER'S TALE

"Some rise by sin, and some by virtue fall":
Why character arcs matter.

*T*HE WINTER'S TALE IS NOT ONE OF SHAKESPEARE'S most popular plays, but it is certainly one of the more interesting. The story begins with the accusations of a brutally jealous husband, and ends with him begging forgiveness from everyone in his family. The play highlights the uniquely human capacity to grow, change, and learn from our mistakes — and it does so through the use of the character arc.

Why are character arcs such an important element of story? What makes the character arcs in this play so powerful? How can we build compelling arcs into our own stories?

START BIG

When tracking a character arc through a story, the temptation is often to write small, thoughtful changes in the name of subtlety and writerly sophistication. But the truth is that in order to make character arcs work, the changes need to be big. If the point is to show how the character changes for the better, the story needs to open with that character at their absolute worst and move toward their personal best. If it's meant to show the opposite, start with the character at their best and move to their worst. No matter what the character arc, the answer is always: GO BIG.

The character arc for Leontes in the *The Winter's Tale* is anything but subtle. The play begins on the day Leontes decides that his wife, Hermione, is cheating on him with his best friend. It's not a slow, careful rumination on adultery, either: within two hundred lines, Leontes works himself into a lather. By the end of the sequence, Leontes disavows his wife, questions whether or not he's really his young son's father, makes plans to kill his unborn child, and orders his trusted advisor to murder his best friend. It is, without a doubt, Leontes at his absolute worst. The play wastes no time setting up this character for change — it's big, and it happens fast.

Like *The Winter's Tale*, the movie *American History X* (1998) begins with a character at his absolute worst. At the end of the first major sequence, Neo-Nazi skinhead Derek (Edward Norton) murders three black men in a brutal scene that ends with Derek telling one of the wounded men to open his mouth and put it on the curb, and with a gruesome smile, crushes the man's skull with the stomp of his boot. The indelible image is horrifying. It is the epitome of going big with a character.

EARN IT

If the character is going to change, the audience needs to see exactly how and why it happens. Otherwise, there's no reason for audiences to believe the change. In tales where the character has something to atone for, for instance, the audience wants to see them suffer before receiving redemption. Characters must earn their transformation.

After Leontes accuses his wife and best friend of betrayal, he loses everything he cares about. His young son, stricken with grief over the accusations against his mother, dies. The newborn child that Leontes rejected has been taken away to be killed. His best friend — the one Leontes had planned to murder — escapes with the help of Leontes' own trusted advisor. Then, his wife Hermione dies. By the midpoint, Leontes has nothing left. He repents his actions, but it's too late — he is completely alone with his grief. That's when his suffering begins:

> *Bring me*
> *To the dead bodies of my queen and son:*
> *One grave shall be for both: upon them shall*
> *The causes of their death appear, unto*
> *Our shame perpetual. Once a day I'll visit*
> *The chapel where they lie, and tears shed there*

Shall be my recreation: so long as nature
Will bear up with this exercise, so long
I daily vow to use it. Come and lead me
Unto these sorrows. (Act 3, scene 2)

It's not enough for Leontes to *say* he's sorry. The audience needs to *see* him grieve in order to believe that he regrets his actions. Leontes earns his transformation through the act of building a shrine and doing nothing but visit that shrine every day — and for no fewer than sixteen years. This is more than a minor shift in character; it's a striking change.

Time is, of course, an important ingredient in change. This is nowhere more clear than in the classic comedy *Groundhog Day* (1993). Unlike Leontes, Phil Connors (Bill Murray) is not atoning for grievous sins like murder and betrayal but rather for the more minor infraction of being a pompous prick. Clearly, the tone of this movie is very different from *The Winter's Tale*, but the deep structures for the character arcs are exactly the same: Phil must earn his transformation by showing the audience what he learns and why it matters. Day by day, we watch as Phil gets to know the people in town, finds ways to help others, listens to and eventually understands the woman he loves, and generally becomes a better person. Phil emerges from the vicious cycle of living the same day over and over again when his transformation is complete — and the audience buys it because they have been there every step of the way.

REDEMPTION (OR NOT)

Not every character gets redeemed at the end of the story. But when you set a goal for a character, the audience needs to see them either achieve that goal, or try and fail. If the character has suffered during the course of the story, then they have earned the chance to seek redemption.

It's not clear if Leontes is redeemed at the end of *The Winter's Tale*. After sixteen years of solitude and grief, he learns that Perdita, the newborn daughter he ordered to be killed, has not only survived but returned to his kingdom. Of course, the first thing Perdita wants to do is see her mother's grave. Hermione's best friend, Paulina, offers to take both Perdita and Leontes to a statue of Hermione that has recently been placed at the gravesite. What happens then is almost too incredible for words. As Perdita and Leontes mourn, the statue moves — it's *alive*. Then we get the reveal: Hermione did not, in fact, die; she was hidden away by her friend Paulina for all those years.

Throughout the scene, Leontes professes his undying love for Hermione, his grief over her loss, and his regret for slandering her pure soul. At one point he even tries to kiss the statue — the measure of his desperate suffering. The scene is painful to watch as Leontes unravels, overwhelmed with joy and sorrow at the same time. If the goal was to make Leontes suffer enough to be worthy of his faithful wife, then this scene achieves it.

Interestingly, however, Hermione does not respond to Leontes' frantic pleas for forgiveness. The only words Hermione speaks are to her daughter, and when she explains why she tricked everyone into believing she was dead, she claims that her only goal was to "preserve" herself to see the child. The ending is left deliberately ambiguous as to whether or not Leontes gains redemption. What's important is that we get to see him try to win redemption, even if he ultimately fails to gain the forgiveness he has pined for the last sixteen years.

Léon: The Professional (1994) offers the audience an unqualified redemption for its protagonist, a hit man named Leon (Jean Reno). Leon begins as a secluded hit man, but when the family of a young neighbor girl is brutally slaughtered by a corrupt DEA agent, he takes her in and reluctantly teaches her his trade. Over the course of the movie Leon and Mathilda (Natalie Portman) become emotionally close — so close, in fact, that when Mathilda decides to take revenge against the DEA agent who killed her family, Leon rushes to save her. In the final scene, Leon sacrifices himself to make sure Mathilda remains safe. Leon, who has lived a life of murder, atones for his sins with his life.

Léon: The Professional, © 1994 Columbia, All Rights Reserved.

KEY POINTS TO REMEMBER

† In order to make character arcs work, the changes need to be BIG.

† If the character is going to change, the audience needs to see exactly how and why it happens.

† When you set a goal for a character, the audience needs to see the character either achieve that goal, or try and fail.

MOVIES TO WATCH

Groundhog Day (1993)
Léon: The Professional (1994)
American History X (1998)

EXERCISES

1. Take a real life hero, either living or dead, and list the positive qualities that he or she has. Now create a character that has the *opposite* characteristics. What changes would the hero need to go through in order to gain those positive attributes? Can you imagine a storyline that would allow for these changes?

2. Almost everyone has experienced a life-changing, "never going to do that again" moment. Write a two-page scene based on your own experience. Show us who you were before, and how and why the moment changed you forever.

3. Most of us have a flaw. Take your own personal flaw and imagine a radical change in which you overcome this flaw. How would you do it? What steps would you need to take? How would overcoming this flaw change your life?

Chapter Twelve

ANTONY AND CLEOPATRA

"All the world's a stage":
Setting isn't just background.

ANTONY AND CLEOPATRA IS ONE OF THE FEW Shakespearean plays in which the setting is as much a part of the story as the main characters. It tells a grand story of forbidden love, but the play is remembered as much for its depictions of the exotic opulence of ancient Egypt as it is for its love story.

Setting is, of course, an important part of every story. But in the richest stories, the setting helps shape the hero, the story, and the conflict. It imbues the narrative with a mood and tone unique to the surroundings. It haunts the audience with indelible images. The setting can be more than just background — it can become a powerful part of the tale.

How does *Antony and Cleopatra* use setting? How does that setting affect the hero, the story, and the conflict? How can we harness the power of the setting in our own scripts?

SHAPING THE HERO

All heroes are the product of their surroundings on some level, but in certain scenarios, their surroundings radically alter their character. When heroes fail to adapt to a new setting, we call it a "fish-out-of-water" story; when they adapt well, it's a story about "going native." In both cases, it is the *setting* that gives shape to the hero and his story.

Antony and Cleopatra is about the dangers of "going native." The hero, Marc Antony, was once a great Roman general. Brave, clever, and valiant — Antony was known as the protector of Rome. But when we find him, he is hanging on the arm of Cleopatra, surrounded by the wealth of Egypt. When Antony enters the court, Philo snickers: "The triple pillar of the world transformed into strumpet's fool: behold and see." Though his friends try to jar Antony back into his old self with news of uprisings against Rome, Antony stubbornly refuses to care:

> *Let Rome in Tiber melt, and the wide arch*
> *Of the ranged empire fall! Here is my space.*
> *Kingdoms are clay: our dungy earth alike*
> *Feeds beast as man: the nobleness of life*
> *Is to do thus.*
>   *(He embraces her)* (Act I, scene I)

Antony has acclimated to his new sumptuous surroundings too well. Cared for as the darling of the Egyptian queen, Antony has gone soft.

Shakespeare begins the play with a discussion of Antony's transformation because he wants us to see that the setting, and everything it encompasses, has dramatically changed Antony. What's more, Antony prefers his new situation. Antony has gone native — and it suits neither him nor those he should be protecting. "These strong Egyptian fetters I must break," he finally intones, "or lose myself in dotage."

Setting likewise shapes the hero in *Lawrence of Arabia* (1962). In this tale, however, going native proves to be a wild and wonderful adventure. The movie follows the transformation of T. E. Lawrence (Peter O'Toole) from an ordinary Englishman into a revolutionary Bedouin leader. The transformation begins when Lawrence suggests crossing the Nefud desert, considered impassable even by the Bedouin. But he persists, surviving the journey through wind-blown sandy deserts, and coming out the other side a new man. No longer truly an Englishman, Lawrence becomes one with the setting — part Bedouin, part legend. By the time he's captured by the Turks, he's nearly unrecognizable. The only remnants of who he used to be are his stunning blue eyes. In this movie, the setting doesn't destroy the man; it creates a remarkable hero — one shaped by the desert he inhabits.

Shaping the Mood and Tone

Not only can the setting change the nature of characters, it can also set the mood and tone for the story. When that setting is original or unusual, it enriches the story with a unique flavor, setting the story apart and making it memorably distinct.

What makes *Antony and Cleopatra* absolutely unforgettable is its depiction of the exotic opulence of ancient Egypt. In one scene after the next, the play delivers images of exorbitant luxury laden with sex and mystery. The inimitable appeal of ancient Egypt blends with the romance between Antony and Cleopatra to produce an intoxicating mix — for Antony, as well as the audience. Egypt is absolutely essential to the tone, mood, and flavor of this famous tale. It couldn't be set anywhere else. Without ancient Egypt, it would be just another love story.

Like *Antony and Cleopatra*, the movie *3:10 to Yuma* (2007) chooses a distinctive setting: the American West. *3:10 to Yuma* fits squarely into the Western genre, which is known for capitalizing on natural scenery to create a unique mood and tone. In fact, the "Wild West," with all its rugged mountain terrain, rocky vistas, and ghost towns, is so pervasive and prominent in Westerns that it almost becomes an extra character. The setting is absolutely inextricable from the mood, tone, and flavor of these stories — its scenery so powerful that it shapes how audiences both imagine and remember the whole genre.

3:10 to Yuma, © 2007 Lionsgate, All Rights Reserved.

SHAPING THE CONFLICT

Not only can the setting help shape the story, it can also shape the nature of the conflict within the story. In some cases, the setting *is* the conflict, and the hero struggles against natural elements to pursue his or her goal. By making whatever challenges the hero faces just that much more difficult, the setting can increase the tension — and payoff — of the story.

In *Antony and Cleopatra*, Antony is drawn into a dispute between Octavius, Pompey, and Lepidus, all of whom want control of the Roman Empire. War erupts as Antony languishes in the Egyptian court. By the time he finally decides to attack, he realizes that he must first master the natural elements of Cairo: namely, water. Antony is used to land wars, but Cleopatra's strength — and her army — rests on the Nile. In his first attempt, Antony almost wins the naval battle, but he loses at the last moment. The second time he incurs a mutiny of the Egyptian navy. Antony loses the battle, and with it, the war for Rome. The natural elements, the exotic luxury of Egypt, the opulent dotage of Queen Cleopatra all come together to ruin Antony. Undone, he kills himself.

As in *Antony and Cleopatra*, the setting works to corrupt the souls of men in *Apocalypse Now* (1979). During the Vietnam War, Captain Benjamin Willard (Martin Sheen) is tasked with finding and killing the wayward Colonel Kurtz (Marlon Brando). As Willard hunts Kurtz, he struggles against the jungle as much as he does the true enemy: the Viet Cong. The jungle becomes a place of confusion, darkness, and insanity. The further Willard travels into the jungle, the more his mind and soul deteriorate. But he is not alone in his madness. The most jarring moment of the film occurs when Lieutenant Colonel Kilgore (Robert Duvall) hunts for a good place to surf during a forward attack, gleefully musing "I love the smell of Napalm in the morning." The moment is deliberately grotesque — designed to show Kilgore's disregard for the pain and suffering inherent in the wartime setting. In the end, the setting overtakes every single major character in the story in the end, leaving all of them either broken or dead.

Apocalypse Now, © 1979 Paramount, All Rights Reserved.

KEY POINTS TO REMEMBER

† Use distinct settings to help shape your hero.

† When a setting is particularly interesting, it enriches the story with a unique flavor, making the story memorably distinct.

† The setting can increase the tension — and payoff — of the story by making whatever challenges the hero faces just that much more daunting.

MOVIES TO WATCH

Lawrence of Arabia (1962)
Apocalypse Now (1979)
3:10 to Yuma (2007)

EXERCISES

1. Take your three favorite movies and set them in a different time and place. How does the change in setting affect the character, plot, mood, and tone?

2. Think back to your favorite vacation. Use the place you visited as the setting for a story that could be told nowhere else. Write up a one-page outline.

3.   Man versus setting. Think up a character. Now imagine the worst possible setting for that character (such as an unsentimental Marine at a ballet recital, or Woody Allen in a war zone). Write up a two-page scene in which the character tries to flee the setting but can't get away.

Chapter Thirteen

MUCH ADO ABOUT NOTHING

"Brevity is the soul of wit":
How to write comedy that's actually funny.

M*UCH ADO ABOUT NOTHING* WAS FIRST STAGED over five hundred year ago. It contains references to a culture that's long gone. And it's written in an antiquated form of English that most people have trouble reading without a dictionary. Yet, the play is one of the funniest that Shakespeare wrote.

What makes this play so comical? How does it manage to be funny across time and place? What's the magic of Shakespeare's humor?

SNARKY ONE-LINERS

One of the reasons Shakespeare's humor works is because it taps into the fundamental, everlasting core of comedy: the insult. From the playground on, nothing tickles the funny bone like a good ribbing.

The insults fly hard and fast between Benedick and Beatrice in *Much Ado About Nothing*. The so-called "merry war" of their relationship consists mainly of trading snide barbs:

> BENEDICK: *I am loved of all ladies, only you excepted. I would I could find in my heart that I had not a hard heart, for truly I love none.*
> BEATRICE: *A dear happiness to women; they would else have been troubled with a pernicious suitor. I thank God and my cold blood I am of your humor for that: I had rather hear my dog bark at a crow than a man swear he loves me.*
> BENEDICK: *God keep your ladyship still in that mind, so some gentleman or other shall escape a predestinate scratched face.*
> BEATRICE: *Scratching could not make it worse, if 'twere such a face as yours were.* (Act I, scene I)

The fun of the scene is in the exchange: as they trade insults, each builds on the other. The jibes become increasingly mean by turn: what starts as an indirect dig — that Benedick does not love Beatrice — ends with Beatrice straight-up calling Benedick ugly. The joke is ultimately on them: they end up falling madly in love by the end.

Snarky one-liners are a fixture in modern comedies, and few are better than those written by Woody Allen. In *Annie Hall* (1977), the audience is treated to a host of witticisms, quips, and snappy comebacks. Unlike the jibes in *Much Ado About Nothing*, however, Allen's insults are mostly aimed at himself. Watch how the insults move in this exchange between Annie and Alvy:

> ALVY: *You're having an affair with your college professor, with that jerk that teaches that incredible crap course, Contemporary Crisis in Western Man.*
> ANNIE: *Existential Motifs in Russian Literature. You're really close.*
> ALVY: *What's the difference? It's all mental masturbation.*
> ANNIE: *Oh, well, now we're finally getting to a subject you know something about.*
> ALVY: *Hey, don't knock masturbation. It's sex with someone I love.*

Alvy brings up masturbation, and Annie attempts to insult him by suggesting he does it a lot. Alvy's response is not to deny that he masturbates, or even to insult her back, but rather to fire off a self-deprecating comeback in which he admits to masturbating. As with *Much Ado About Nothing*, the genius of this exchange between Annie and Alvy is in the progression: the jibes become increasingly mean as they near the punch line — and the result is a comedy gold.

IDIOTS

Everybody loves watching idiots make fools of themselves. Shakespeare must've realized this: in every play he wrote, Shakespeare added at least one idiot, fool, or clown — including in his tragedies. Idiots are a crowd-pleasing building block of comedy.

In *Much Ado About Nothing*, we get a world-class idiot in the town watchman, Dogberry. Dim-witted but well-meaning, Dogberry has a habit of misusing similar-sounding words, or what's called a *malapropism.* For example, when Dogberry laments that "comparisons are odorous," he means they're *odious*, not smelly. Dogberry is untroubled by such details — he blasts full steam ahead, and, near the middle of the play, actually does succeed in apprehending two "arrant knaves." Thrilled, Dogberry presents them to the town governor, Leonato. What follows is a conversation filled with garbled language and misunderstandings. Frustrated, Leonato interrupts Dogberry:

> LEONATO: *Neighbors, you are tedious.*
> DOGBERRY: *It pleases your worship to say so, but we are the poor duke's officers; but truly, for mine own part, if I were as tedious as a king, I could find it in my heart to bestow it all of your worship.*
> LEONATO: *All thy tediousness on me?*
> DOGBERRY: Y*ea, if 'twere a thousand pound more than 'tis.* (Act 3, scene 5)

Dogberry clearly has no idea what "tedious" means, nor that it does not cost money, but that doesn't stop him from using the word in a sentence. What's funny about Dogberry is that he hopes to sound smart, but keeps missing the mark. It's the intention, as much as the failure, that draws laughs.

Yet, Dogberry serves an important function in the play. Not only is his lack of facility with language a foil for the extreme wit of Benedick and Beatrice, Dogberry also ends up saving the day by catching the criminals who falsely slandered the character Hero. Without Dogberry, the play would've ended as a tragedy. His idiocy is surpassed only by his capacity to do good.

Like Dogberry, Buddy in *Elf* (2003) is a dim-witted but lovable guy, and like Dogberry, Buddy ends up saving the day at the end of the movie. The movie begins with Buddy (Will Ferrell), a human raised as an elf at the North Pole, being sent to New York City to find his real father. Of course, being in the big city is a shock to Buddy — and it causes one misunderstanding after the next. If Buddy isn't accidentally insulting a little person by calling him an "angry elf," he's outing the department store Santa as a fake ("You smell like beef and cheese, you don't smell like Santa!"). Through it all, Buddy is unflaggingly cheerful and obliging. As with Dogberry, it's the combination of foolishness with good-heartedness that makes Buddy so funny — and so appealing — as a character.

Elf, © 2003 New Line, All Rights Reserved.

HUMILIATING SITUATIONS

Humiliation is fundamental to comedy. Just as audiences love idiots, they love watching characters get humiliated. The greater the humiliation, the bigger the laugh.

This is absolutely true in *Much Ado About Nothing*. After enduring several pompous, long-winded speeches from Benedick on the drawbacks of marriage, Benedick's friends get together and decide to play a trick on him. The friends wait until they see Benedick wandering in the garden. Then, just loud enough for Benedick to hear, they make up all sorts of silly stories about how Beatrice is ready to kill herself for the love of Benedick. Unbelievably, it works — Benedick believes that Beatrice is in love with him. What's more, he is *overjoyed* to hear it. He decides that he will reciprocate her love and be wildly, madly in love with her.

The final part of their trick involves sending Beatrice out to fetch Benedick. Of course, she knows nothing of all this. As she stomps toward him, Benedick licks his lips with anticipation: "I do spy some marks of love in her," he says gleefully. That's when the fun begins:

> BEATRICE: *Against my will I am sent to bid you come in to dinner.*
> BENEDICK: *Fair Beatrice, I thank you for your pains.*
> BEATRICE: *I took no more pains for those thanks than you take pains to thank me. If it had been painful, I would not have come.*
> BENEDICK: *You take pleasure then in the message?*
> BEATRICE: *Yea, just so much as you may take upon a knife's point.*
> (Act 2, scene 3)

Beatrice's surly remarks don't deter Benedick. If anything, it eggs him on. No matter how rude she is, he sees it as proof that she's got the hots for him. As soon as she leaves, he exclaims:

> BENEDICK: *Ha! 'Against my will I am sent to bid you come in to dinner.'*
> *There's a double meaning in that.* (Act 2, scene 3)

Of course, there isn't a double meaning — Beatrice means exactly what she says. Benedick's friends have humiliated him by tricking him into falling for a woman who hates his guts. In this scene, it's the situation that produces the laughs; the painfully awkward conversation is the icing on the cake.

In *There's Something About Mary* (1998), we get two of the funniest awkward moments ever captured on film. In the opening sequence, Ted (Ben Stiller) is supposed to go to the prom with his dream girl, Mary (Cameron Diaz) — but the date is cut short, as it were, when Ted gets his "frank and beans" caught in his zipper. The scene gives new meaning to painful humiliation, but it doesn't end there. Many years later, Ted reconnects with Mary, and even gets her to agree to a date. On a friend's advice, he decides to "choke the chicken" just before they go out. Only, after he does it, he can't find where the semen went. The doorbell rings — and there's Mary. Her smile fades when she sees something hanging from his ear lobe. "Is that... hair gel?" she asks. Before he can answer, she grabs it and smears it into her hair. Both scenes trade on humiliation, but as with *Much Ado About Nothing*, it's the situation, not the dialogue, that generates the big laughs.

KEY POINTS TO REMEMBER

† The fundamental, everlasting core of comedy is the insult; it is one of the surest ways to a laugh.

† Everybody loves watching idiots make fools of themselves.

† Just as audiences love idiots, they love watching characters get humiliated.

MOVIES TO WATCH

Annie Hall (1977)
There's Something About Mary (1998)
Elf (2003)

EXERCISES

1.   Recall a personal embarrassment or humiliation and make it into a two-page scene. How does it begin and end? Is it funny?

2.   Now change that scene, making it a public scandal. What if your humiliating moment were caught on film and uploaded to YouTube? Or witnessed by someone you love or respect? How does that add to the humor of the scene?

3.   Think of your favorite scene in a movie where a character gets humiliated. Can you re-write the scene to take it up a notch?

Chapter Fourteen

THE MERCHANT OF VENICE

"If you prick us, do we not bleed":
The more your characters suffer, the better.

*T*HE MERCHANT OF VENICE IS WHAT Shakespeare scholars consider to be a "problem play." The issue is that, though Shylock is
technically the villain, he is also a tremendously sympathetic character. In fact, the speech most people remember from the play belongs
to Shylock ("If you prick us, do we not bleed?"). Problematically,
Shylock does not fit the stereotypical mold for antagonists.

The Merchant of Venice is a masterful example of creating sympathy
for all sides, both good and bad, and it does so by making every single
one of the characters suffer. Suffering humanizes your characters and
deepens the audience's connection to them. That connection is particularly powerful when the audience sympathizes not only with the
hero but also with the villain. Through its use of suffering, *The Merchant of Venice* adds layer after layer of emotional complexity as it draws
the audience into its narrative. In other words, it's exactly the kind of
"problem" you want to have in your stories.

What makes the suffering so powerful in this drama? And how
can we capture its power in our own scripts?

HARD CHOICES

Characters are determined by their choices. What does the character want? How far will that character go tos get it? What are they
willing to sacrifice? The harder the choices, the more character suffers,
becoming more complexly human in the process.

Difficult choices are at the heart of *The Merchant of Venice.* In the
first scene, Bassanio confides to his best friend Antonio that he is in
love with Portia. Unfortunately, Bassanio is too poor to venture to

Colchis, where she lives, to win her hand. Portia is beset by suitors, so if Bassanio doesn't find the money to visit soon, he will lose her. Antonio wants to help, but his fortune is locked up in ongoing ventures, so he offers to help Bassanio by acting as surety on a loan. The two ask Shylock, a moneylender, to make the loan.

Shylock initially refuses their request for a loan. He hates Antonio, who regularly curses him and spits at him because Shylock is a Jew. But Shylock is without other income, so he eventually agrees, on one condition. Taunting Antonio, Shylock demands that if the loan isn't repaid in three months' time, he will be entitled to one pound of flesh from Antonio. In other words, if they don't pay up, Shylock will take Antonio's life.

Life, death, love, vengeance. Each choice these characters make rages with emotion. Bassanio agrees out of desperation. Antonio agrees out of anti-Semitic spite. Shylock agrees out of need and the tantalizing prospect of revenge. There is nothing easy or simple about these choices. The characters are fully boxed in to their decisions — and their responses come alive with uniquely human feeling.

The Hunger Games (2012) takes life and death choices to the extreme. The movie features a dystopian, post-apocalyptic state called Panem. As punishment for a past rebellion, Panem decrees that two children from each of the twelve districts will fight to the death in a yearly event called the "Hunger Games." Entering the area as the "tribute" for her district, Katniss (Jennifer Lawrence) is thrown into a horrific situation in which she either kills or gets killed. When she starts to have feelings for one of her fellow tributes, Peeta (Josh Hutcherson), things become even more complicated. At the climax of the movie, it's down to Katniss and Peeta, who must either kill one another or die. Could you kill someone you love to survive? Would you sacrifice your life for them? The story takes hard choices and gives them a knife's edge. The thrill of watching the characters suffer through their anguished decisions made the movie a box office smash and inspired a fevered following among teen viewers.

BETRAYAL

Everyone has been betrayed at one point or another. It's a painful experience, especially when it comes from someone you know and love. Because everyone understands betrayal, this unique brand of suffering is highly relatable and makes for great drama. A betrayal can create or destroy sympathy for a character, transforming our fundamental notions of who the characters truly are.

This is never more true than with the character of Shylock. Near the middle of the play, Shylock's daughter Jessica elopes with her boyfriend, Lorenzo. Not only does Jessica leave, she steals Shylock's money and jewels. Shylock is abandoned by his only child. Adding insult to injury, his Christian counterparts knew about it and didn't tell him. Instead, they laugh at him and make fun of his pain. Nearly destroyed, Shylock launches into one of the more poignant speeches in Shakespeare's work:

> *Hath not a Jew eyes? Hath not a Jew hands, organs,*
> *dimensions, senses, affections, passions? Fed with*
> *the same food, hurt with the same weapons, subject*
> *to the same diseases, healed by the same means,*
> *warmed and cooled by the same winter and summer, as*
> *a Christian is? If you prick us, do we not bleed?* (Act 3, scene I)

Shylock's plea for tolerance is affecting: Jews and Christians are not truly different; we are all human. Against a backdrop of anti-Semitism in this play, and despite the fact that he is the villain, it is

Shylock's suffering that resonates — so much so, that the most frequently quoted and remembered lines of the play are these powerful lines given to Shylock.

Betrayal is a common theme in modern cinema, but the film that sets the bar for all movies on the topic is the classic *All About Eve* (1950). It tells the story of Margo, an aging actress, who befriends a lonely drifter, Eve. Though Eve seems all sweetness and adoration, she subtly works behind the scenes to supplant Margo: driving a wedge between Margo and her friends, attempting to seduce Margo's boyfriend, even becoming the understudy in Margo's play. Using Margo's friends, Eve eventually blackmails her way onto the big stage, and the betrayal is complete — or so we think, until the chilling last scene, when Eve, now a big star, gets a devious "devotee" of her own.

RECKONING

If your characters are complex, the good ones will have made some bad decisions and the bad characters some good ones. The moment when the characters are called to account for their actions, both good and bad, is the reckoning. The harsher the reckoning, the stronger the climax.

The reckoning in *The Merchant of Venice* involves all three main characters. Bassanio has won the hand of Portia, but Antonio and Bassanio have been unable to pay their debt to Shylock within the agreed timeframe. Though Portia offers to pay three times the full amount in back payment, Shylock refuses. He wants the pound of flesh from Antonio. Nothing else will do.

The terror of the moment is palpable. Antonio will lose his life — and Bassanio will be forced to watch his friend die. All the hard choices they made at the beginning of the play come back to haunt them.

At the last minute, Portia, incognito as the judge, comes up with a save. She decrees that Shylock may take his pound of flesh, but the contract says nothing about blood. If Shylock draws blood, he will be killed on the spot. The tide turns rapidly at this point in the play, and it's Shylock's time to pay. Shylock changes his mind and asks for the money instead, but it's too late. Portia negates the debt and accuses Shylock of attempted murder. As Shylock begs for his life, they drag him away. The punishment is excessive, and the villain of the play is once again humanized in this starkly affecting reckoning.

Like *The Merchant of Venice*, the reckoning in *L.A. Confidential* (1997) is radically intense. The three main characters, Bud (Russell Crowe), Exley (Guy Pearce), and Jack (Kevin Spacey), are all basically good guys who have made bad choices. Exley lies to get a promotion to Detective; Jack feels responsible for the death of a young kid in Hollywood; Bud, in a fit of jealous rage, hits his girlfriend. All of them have something to atone for at the end of the movie. Just before the final sequence, Bud and Exley team up to take on the villain. It's a suicide mission, but they know that they need to pay for their crimes — and they want to go down swinging. In the cataclysmic climax, Bud and Exley atone for their offenses with blood and anguish. They make it out alive, but only just. Their suffering makes the reckoning complete.

In both *The Merchant of Venice* and *L.A. Confidential*, every single major character is called to account for their choices. The result is a climax that is harsh, painful — and thrilling.

L.A. Confidential, © 1997 Warner Bros., All Rights Reserved.

Key Points to Remember

† Use suffering to create sympathy for your characters.

† Suffering humanizes your characters and deepens the audience's connection to them.

† The best stories create sympathy not only for the hero but also the villain.

† Let your characters come to terms with the pain, the hard choices, and the suffering in a final, climactic reckoning.

Movies to Watch

All About Eve (1950)
L.A. Confidential (1997)
The Hunger Games (2012)

Exercises

1. There are millions of ways characters can suffer. Choose one particular kind of suffering, such as loss, betrayal, or defeat, and build a character around it. What does the character want? How does their suffering affect their goals, motivations, and choices? How might that character come to terms with that suffering?

2. Characters are about choices. If you've got a script you're currently working on, or a backlog you'd like to revise, go through your story and list out all the choices your protagonist had to make. Are they hard choices? Did they make your protagonist suffer? Was your protagonist forced to reckon with the consequences of those choices at the end? Now take a look at your antagonist. Do you provide a rationale for why they do what they do? Do you create sympathy for the character? Think of ways you could add to the character's emotional complexity and relatability by making them suffer.

3. Pick your favorite villain, from Darth Vader to Norman Bates. Write a diary entry from their point of view about the most painful moment in their lives. For instance, how did Vader feel when Luke screamed out in utter despair when he learned Vader was his father? Focus on finding the pain — it is the root of emotional complexity.

PART II

THE
BIG
PICTURE

Chapter Fifteen

How Shakespeare creates unforgettable heroes:

Hamlet, Henry V, and Othello.

When most people think of heros, they think of words like courage, bravery, wisdom, strength, honor, and integrity. These are the qualities we imagine we want from a "hero." But if you look through Shakespeare's work, there is not a single hero with these qualities.

Shakespeare knew that real heroes — the ones that truly move us — are far from perfect. Why? Because most of us are imperfect beings. We like our heroes a little bit broken because we are, too. It is a simple psychological truth: audiences aren't inspired by watching perfect heroes triumph in small battles. They're inspired by watching imperfect humans struggle to do great things.

This chapter dissects three of Shakespeare's most memorable heroes — Henry V, Hamlet, and Othello — to discover what makes them so compelling.

Make Your Hero An Underdog

There are few variations on a hero as popular as the underdog. Watching a hero struggle to overcome nearly insurmountable odds is one of the purest narrative pleasures ever conceived. Absolutely everyone loves an underdog.

Henry V is a classic underdog, and one of Shakespeare's most revered heroes as a result. Henry starts out as a young, unproven king with a sordid past. He's never even been to a war, let alone won one, so when he and his ragtag army of Englishman end up on the edge of the biggest battle of their lifetimes, they are terrified. They should be — they're outnumbered twenty-five to one! Inexperienced, and severely outnumbered, Henry is a true underdog. But he rises to the occasion, inspiring his troops with the rousing St. Crispin's Day speech, and against all odds the English manage to win. The dazzling, come-from-behind victory keeps audiences nailed to their seats. It is everything an underdog story should be.

The underdog hero translates particularly well to the silver screen. One of the greatest underdog films of all time, *Rocky* (1976) tells the story of a small-time boxer who ends up fighting World Heavyweight Champion Apollo Creed. At the start of the film, Rocky (Sylvester Stallone) can hardly make it through a single practice. But he is determined to make it. In the most famous sequence from the film, Rocky races up the steps in Philadelphia to a soundtrack that has become synonymous with overcoming the odds. It is a thrilling moment, one designed to make the audience cheer for the under-dog hero. What most people don't remember about the film is that Rocky's goal is not to win the fight against Creed, but rather to go fifteen rounds. In fact, Rocky doesn't actually win at the end. It's a sweet success nevertheless, because Rocky proves once and for all that he's not "just another bum from the neighborhood," but rather a true hero capable of rising above. Both Rocky and Henry V become memorable heroes not because they were born with innate honor, but because they managed to overcome their imperfections.

Rocky, © 1976 MGM, All Rights Reserved.

Give Your Hero a Weak Spot

Othello is an extraordinary character. Not only is he a successful black man living in the white world of Venice, he's an incomparable warrior and a revered military tactician. More than that, he's a wise leader, a true friend, and a honorable man. Othello is the very definition of heroism, with one important exception: he has a weak spot. Vulnerable to the "green-eyed monster," Othello is a deeply jealous man.

Supervillain Iago is keenly aware of Othello's blind spot and uses it to his advantage. Through scams and machinations, Iago convinces Othello that Desdemona is having extra-marital relations with another man. Instead of proceeding logically and questioning Iago, Othello instantly and whole-heartedly believes the lies, flying into a jealous rage so powerful it ends with Othello sneaking into his wife's bedchamber and suffocating her to death with his bare hands. It's a horribly cruel trick that destroys more than one life — and all because Othello can't control his feelings of jealousy.

What makes Othello a compelling character is not his heroic nature but rather his weak spot. Everyone knows what it feels like to be driven crazy with jealousy. Because the audience can relate to his jealous fears, Othello becomes a kind of Everyman character. He is the classic hero undone by his own weakness, and we love it because we can imagine the scenario happening to us.

Black Swan (2010) tells the story of Nina (Natalie Portman), a young dancer with the New York City ballet, who wins the coveted

Black Swan, © 2010 20th Century Fox, All Rights Reserved.

part of the Swan Queen. As we soon learn, however, Nina is plagued by crippling perfectionism. The more she pushes herself, the more her mental health deteriorates. In the final sequence, Nina's weak spot consumes her: she gives a spectacular performance, but it ends with her self-destruction. "I just wanted it to be perfect," she says.

We all have a weak spot, no matter what it is, and these stories make the idea of being conquered by our weakness seem like a terrifyingly realistic possibility.

HAVE YOUR HERO DO THE WRONG THING FOR THE RIGHT REASONS

The most famous of all Shakespeare's "heroes" is without a doubt Hamlet. Far from a typical hero, however, Hamlet is actually best known for waffling on decisions. What makes Hamlet fascinating is that when he does act, he does the wrong thing for the right reasons.

For example, when Hamlet finally decides that Claudius is guilty and should be killed, he goes to kill him. Claudius happens to be sitting in a church at that moment. Hamlet mistakenly believes that Claudius is praying, and reasons that it's probably not a good idea to kill someone praying in a church, given that it could send his soul to eternal damnation. Just after Hamlet leaves, the audience hears Claudius admit that he doesn't even feel sorry for killing Hamlet's father. Claudius is a wicked villain and deserves to die. More than that, he will shortly turn dangerous, attempting to kill both Hamlet and Hamlet's mother, Gertrude. Hamlet clearly makes the wrong decision in foregoing the murder, but he does so because he believes in something bigger than himself: the everlasting judgment of the Almighty. That belief is a good reason to make the wrong decision.

We've all made mistakes. Some of us have even made mistakes while trying to do the right thing. Watching Hamlet do so triggers our sympathy even as we criticize his decisions. What we can learn from Hamlet, then, is two-fold. First, audiences sympathize with characters who struggle to do the right thing, even if they make mistakes. Second, the paradoxical nature of doing the wrong thing for the right reasons adds a layer of complexity to your hero while simultaneously building your hero's personal integrity, because your hero has followed his heart, even if the audience knows he shouldn't have.

Listed as having one of the greatest film heroes of all time by the American Film Institute, *Serpico* (1973) tells the story of a cop who goes undercover to expose corruption in the police force. Harassed and threatened by fellow cops, and facing the complete destruction of his personal life, Frank Serpico (Al Pacino) doggedly refuses to give up his investigation. He is the opposite of Hamlet: he never waffles. But that's actually the problem: even when the costs start to outweigh the benefits, Serpico refuses to back down. He is absolutely relentless in his pursuit of truth. Like Hamlet, Serpico does the wrong thing for the right reasons. He makes mistakes in the service of a good idea. The result is a complex, dynamic, and unforgettable hero.

KEY POINTS TO REMEMBER

† Everyone loves an underdog; watching a hero struggle to overcome nearly insurmountable odds is one of the purest narrative pleasures ever conceived.

† Give your hero a weak spot to make them more relatable.

† Have your hero do the wrong thing for the right reasons.

† Audiences sympathize with characters who struggle to do the right thing, even if they mistakes.

MOVIES TO WATCH

Serpico (1973)
Rocky (1976)
Black Swan (2010)

EXERCISES

I. Pick a Goliath in this world. Then imagine the puniest David to take them down. In ten action lines, craft a story that explains how your David defeats your Goliath.

2.   What is your own personal weak spot? Create a character around that weak spot, amplifying the weakness by a hundred. Can you imagine a storyline in which the character would overcome his or her own weakness? Or be consumed by it?

3.   Think of the most heinous crime you can imagine. Now challenge yourself to create a good reason for a character to do such a bad thing. Why has your hero done the wrong thing for the right reasons?

Chapter Sixteen

REVERSE ENGINEERING SHAKESPEARE'S SUPERVILLAINS:

Iago, Macbeth, and *Richard III.*

EVERYONE KNOWS YOU NEED A GOOD HERO in your script. As writers we spend hours giving them intriguing back stories, inspiring goals, and delicious flaws. It is an art, and one that every screenwriter must master. What most people don't know is that the true secret to a good hero is a good villain. Why? Because the purpose of a hero is to face down a challenge. If that challenge isn't substantial, then the movie goes soft. Your villain must be smarter, sexier, and more successful than your hero.

Shakespeare wrote some of the most terrifying and memorable villains ever committed to paper. What makes Shakespeare's villains uniquely frightening? What makes them unforgettable? This chapter dissects three of Shakespeare's supervillains — Iago, Macbeth, and Richard III — to discover what makes these characters tick.

IAGO

The *why* of a character is their motive — and for villains, motive is everything. Yet, one of Shakespeare's more harrowing villains, Iago, is most famous for *not* having a motive. Why did Shakespeare create a villain without a motive? And why is it so effective?

The question of Iago's motive is one that critics have puzzled over for years. In 1874, famed poet Samuel Taylor Coleridge wrote a long diatribe on the nature of Iago's evil and why it was so frightening for audiences, arguing that it is Iago's "motiveless malignity" that truly disturbs us. We are far more frightened, he argues, by a malice that is has no apparent source or pattern.

Because we never find out why Iago betrays and tricks Othello into killing Desdemona, we are left with more questions than answers. Our fundamental human desire to learn the source of malice goes unanswered. Shakespeare must have known this would scare audiences. The final lines from Iago in the play are in response to a direct question from Othello:

> OTHELLO. *Will you, I pray, demand that demi-devil*
> *Why he hath thus ensnared my soul and body?*
> IAGO. *Demand of me nothing. What you know, you know.*
> *From this time forth, I shall not speak a word.* (Act 5, scene 2)

In the end, Othello only wants to know *why* — and the final twist of the knife is Iago's refusal to reveal this information.

In deceiving Othello, Iago preys on our fear of being duped by someone we know and love. Iago is the devil that we don't even know is after us. We can't anticipate his moves because we have no idea what he wants or why. The lesson here is clear: the villain we don't see coming is far more frightening than the one we do.

By not giving Iago a motive, Shakespeare breaks the rules of convention. The audience is conditioned to expect a motive, which is why we are so shocked. But in this, too, we can find a lesson: the element of surprise matters to audiences. We enjoy novelty almost as much as we enjoy being frightened. The best villains offer the audience something new and unexpected.

Despite the fact that Iago is one of Shakespeare's most popular characters, few writers have attempted to mimic his "motiveless malignity" on the big screen. One notable exception is The Joker in *The Dark Knight* (2008). The Joker (Heath Ledger) is as clever as he is unpredictable: in one terrifying sequence, we are completely caught off guard when The Joker calls in a bomb threat to all the hospitals in Gotham and appears in wounded Harvey Dent's room as a nurse in disguise. We believe The Joker has set up the hospital bombing to kill Harvey Dent, but The Joker is not there to kill Harvey; instead, The Joker offers himself up to be killed. When a flip of the coin gives The Joker his life, The Joker doesn't retaliate or demand anything specific from Harvey; he lets Harvey go — hoping, we learn, that a taste of revenge will turn Harvey from a good guy to a bloodthirsty rogue. It doesn't matter to The Joker who Harvey kills, just as long as he wants to kill.

Like Iago, The Joker has no discernible motive. He is not after wealth or sex: he kidnaps Rachel Dawes only to torture Batman; his alliance with the mob ends when he sets fire to their stores of cash. When he rigs the ferries with bombs as a "social experiment," he offers the riders a chance at survival if they are willing to blow the other ferry up first. Throughout the movie, The Joker is a symbol of chaos and random cruelty. The only thing The Joker hopes to accomplish is evil. As Batman's trusted advisor Alfred puts it: "some men just want to see the world burn."

The Dark Knight, © 2008 Warner Bros., All Rights Reserved.

MACBETH

On the opposite side of the spectrum, the villain most associated with motive is Macbeth. His objective is staggeringly simple: to kill the king and take over the realm of Scotland. It is the essence of driving ambition in its bloodiest form.

Shakespeare structures the play around the inception, fulfillment, and destruction of Macbeth's ambitions. We begin with the witches giving Macbeth the information that will propel his aspirations; then we follow Macbeth as he kills Duncan and takes over his throne; and we end with Macbeth being defeated and killed by Malcolm and Macduff. What is interesting about this is that at the beginning of the play, Macbeth is hailed as a hero. He is a good soldier and a good commander, without any designs on power or kingship. It is only after he meets the witches that Macbeth becomes consumed with the idea that he will become king. Rather than showing us a villain already obsessed with power, Shakespeare allows us to watch Macbeth be seduced. We see the ambition take root and begin to burn his soul. "Full of scorpions is my mind," he howls — as the need for power overtakes him.

Ambition has become one of the most common motives for villains on the big screen. We love to watch our villains be consumed by their own desires — perhaps none more than Gordon Gekko in *Wall Street* (1987). Like Macbeth, Gekko (Michael Douglas) is obsessed with rising to the top. Set in the financial world, Gekko is fixated on money as the sole motivator for his every move. "What's worth doing," he tells us, "is worth doing for money." His passionate pursuit of money culminates in a speech to stockholders — a speech that has since become famous as a touchstone for discussing the ruthless avarice of the 1980s:

> *The point is, ladies and gentleman, that greed, for lack of a better word, is good. Greed is right, greed works. Greed clarifies, cuts through, and captures the essence of the evolutionary spirit. Greed, in all of its forms — greed for life, for money, for love, knowledge — has marked the upward surge of mankind. And greed, you mark my words, will not only save Teldar Paper, but that other malfunctioning corporation called the USA. Thank you very much.*

Gekko surprises us by arguing against expectations: rather than downplaying the negative impact of materialism, he emphatically and unequivocally embraces ambition as a necessary part of progress. Greed is, however, also what lands him in jail by the end of movie.

Villains like Gekko and Macbeth appeal to audiences because they offer us a window into our own soul. The audience is both captivated — and repulsed — by the destructive power of the craven desires they see there.

RICHARD III

Of all Shakespeare's villains, none is more repulsive than Richard III. Richard is a deformed, evil killer — his body as twisted as his soul. And yet, Richard is also one of Shakespeare's most seductive characters. In one remarkable scene, Richard manages to woo a woman while she is standing over the dead body of her husband. It is an astonishing feat of persuasion, and one that has fascinated both audiences and critics alike for hundreds of years.

In the beginning of the scene, Lady Anne mourns over the bodies of her husband and father-in-law, whose deaths she blames on Richard. She curses Richard as a murderer, praying that any child of his be deformed and any woman he marry be miserable. Her state of mind is important, as she will have completely reversed herself by the end of the scene.

When Richard enters, Anne reacts with horror and spite, even going so far as to spit at him. But Richard persists. He chastises Anne for cursing him, reminding her that good Christian charity requires she turn the other cheek. Richard counters every objection that Anne raises with a stronger argument. All of these entreaties Lady Anne resists. What happens next is startling.

Richard confesses to murdering Lady Anne's husband — and declares that he did it because he loves her. This is where the real genius of the scene lies. Richard takes the sting out of her accusations by admitting guilt and claiming that his love for her was the reason. The calculated move leaves Anne at a rhetorical dead end. As she falls silent, Richard drops to one knee. He gives her his sword and offers up his life:

> *Teach not thy lips such scorn, for they were made*
> *For kissing, lady, not for such contempt.*
> *If thy revengeful heart cannot forgive,*
> *Lo, here I lend thee this sharp-pointed sword;*
> *Which if thou please to hide in this true bosom.*
> *And let the soul forth that adoreth thee,*
> *I lay it naked to the deadly stroke,*
> *And humbly beg the death upon my knee.*

(He lays his breast open; she offers at it with his sword)
Nay, do not pause; for I did kill King Henry,
But 'twas thy beauty that provoked me.
Nay, now dispatch; 'twas I that stabb'd young Edward,
But 'twas thy heavenly face that set me on.
(She lets the sword fall)
Take up the sword again, or take up me.

By the end of the speech, Richard traps Anne in a logical fallacy: she can either kill him, or love him. There is no in-between. Lady Anne is unable to kill Richard — more proof of her own goodness than her love for him — but Richard uses the moment to slip a ring onto her finger as a token of his sincere devotion. To our horror, Lady Anne accepts.

The turn of events is extraordinary. In the space of 250 lines, Richard persuades Anne that he is not a bloodthirsty killer but rather a misguided, lovesick man enthralled with her beauty and grace. As soon as Lady Anne is out of the room, of course, we learn the truth. Richard can't help himself — he launches into a gleeful soliloquy, gloating over his accomplishment:

Was ever woman in this humour woo'd?
Was ever woman in this humour won? (Act I, scene 2)

Richard is quick to note that his achievement has little precedence. His powers of persuasion are, in fact, truly sensational here. No matter what the audience thinks of Richard as a person, they are forced to accept that he is a mastermind of manipulation.

Richard III remains one of Shakespeare's most popular villains because he is prodigiously gifted. Audiences want to watch gifted characters, and we want to be seduced by their powers of persuasion. We enjoy being lured in to their traps. The delight audiences take in watching seductive villains like Richard III reveals a fundamental human truth: we are drawn to evil. It is dark, dirty, dangerous — and delicious.

On par with the seductive villainy of Richard III is Hannibal Lecter in *The Silence of the Lambs* (1991). Who can forget the chills down their spine when Lecter (Anthony Hopkins) leans forward and whispers to Clarice Starling, "a census taker tried to test me — I ate his liver with some fava beans and a nice chianti"? He means both to frighten and impress her. The result, for the audience, is thrilling.

Hannibal Lecter's relationship with Clarice is not, of course, romantic in nature, but their relationship is at the heart of the movie. The inciting incident revolves around their first meeting, and the final words of the movie are a phone call from the escaped Lecter to Clarice. In fact, throughout the movie, Lecter attempts to charm Clarice, and by extension the audience, with his unique powers of persuasion. After her first visit, as proof of his admiration, Lecter murders Miggs, the prisoner who insulted Clarice, using nothing but words. Clarice reciprocates by sharing intimate stories of her childhood that one might tell a lover. At one point, Lecter even makes a point of their nascent "romance" after she breaks in to see him: "People will say we're in love, Clarice." Both Richard III and Hannibal Lecter are virtuosos of manipulation: terrifyingly intelligent, and grotesquely alluring in their power to control. Ultimately, it is the audience who is seduced by their powers.

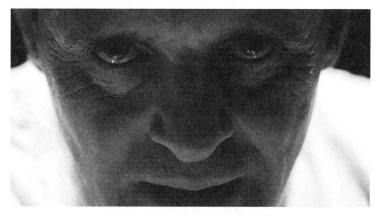

The Silence of the Lambs, © 1991 MGM, All Rights Reserved.

KEY POINTS TO REMEMBER

† Your villain must be smarter, sexier, and more successful than your hero.

† The villain we don't see coming is far more frightening than the one we do.

† The ambitious desire for money, sex, love, or power are among the most common, and relatable, motives for villains.

† Audiences love to watch clever, seductive villains.

MOVIES TO WATCH

Wall Street (1987)
The Silence of the Lambs (1991)
The Dark Knight (2008)

EXERCISES

1. Think of your favorite movie villain. Is that villain smarter, sexier, and more successful than the hero? What makes the villain so seductive? Make a list that compares and contrasts the qualities of the hero and your favorite villain.

2. Everyone is deathly afraid of something. What terrifies you? Betrayal, enclosed spaces, heights, sharks? Create a villain that taps into your own worst fears. What does the villain do? How does he torture people? What does he want? What is he willing to do to get it?

3. Villains are really just distorted shadows of the hero. Both are driven to a particular goal, and both will do whatever it takes to get it. Think of your favorite hero. Now imagine that hero as the villain, and re-tell the story with the roles of hero and villain reversed.

Chapter Seventeen

UNLOCKING THE SECRET TO THE GREATEST LOVE STORY EVER TOLD:

Romeo and Juliet.

Everyone knows that *Romeo and Juliet* is one of the greatest love stories ever written. Even if we haven't read the play, we've been exposed to its sentimental themes. Its timeless premise has been reflected in every medium imaginable, from operas to ballets to animated comedies to Broadway musicals and Oscar-winning dramas. With its wide-reaching appeal, *Romeo and Juliet* represents the very essence of romance.

Yet, for all its romance, *Romeo and Juliet* is a simple story of a boy and a girl. What makes this love story so powerful? What makes it so romantic? What is this story's special magic? And how can we capture that magic in our own stories?

FORBIDDEN FRUIT

At some point in our lives, most of us have been drawn to someone we shouldn't have been drawn to. That attraction is an essential truth of human existence. In terms of story structure, having your characters be attracted to someone forbidden adds an element of thrill by introducing a natural obstacle to the romance.

Shakespeare may not have invented the concept of "forbidden fruit," but he certainly perfected it in *Romeo and Juliet*. In the first lines, we learn that there is a family feud raging in Verona and that Romeo and Juliet are on opposite sides of the battle: one is a Capulet, the other a Montague. Of course, the fact that they are not supposed to be together turns out to be a fundamental part of the attraction. In the scene where Romeo and Juliet first meet, neither has eyes for anyone else except the one they are not supposed to be with. They kiss within seconds of meeting each other, and Juliet exclaims: "My only love sprung from my only hate!" (Act I, scene 5), already swearing undying love. Romeo can't stay away from her — the first thing he does after he's ejected from the Capulet ball is return to her house and watch her at her balcony. Their clandestine night meeting, in which they kiss in the moonlight, is one of the most romantic scenes ever written. The fact that they're doing it against their parents' wishes makes it all the more thrilling. By the next act, they are married and naked in bed.

Using the forbidden fruit formula, James Cameron's *Titanic* (1997) crafts one of the most moving love stories in recent memory. The romance centers on a the poor drifter Jack (Leonardo DiCaprio) and the wealthy Rose (Kate Winslet). Of course, her family aims to keep them apart, but the fact that their love is forbidden actually fuels the fire. As in *Romeo and Juliet*, the romance blossoms hard and fast: the first time they meet, Jack saves Rose from jumping over the side of the boat; by the next night, Jack and Rose escape together, going from their famous kiss at the bow of the ship, to the naked sketching session, to their love-making in the back of a parked car stored in the galley. Their love story is powerful, urgent — and utterly captivating.

A GLIMPSE OF PARADISE

From the start, we know that *Romeo and Juliet* isn't going to end well. But for one brief moment, everything is absolutely perfect. It is a glimpse of paradise. Watching the lovers enjoy pure bliss is utterly intoxicating for the audience, and it is a necessary part of building a compelling romance.

The moment of bliss comes for Romeo and Juliet in a brief scene just after they are married. Romeo has been exiled because he killed Tybalt, a Capulet, and Juliet's cousin. They have exactly one night to spend together before Romeo must leave, which only heightens the intensity. The scene opens in the morning. They've just made love — for the first, last, and only time. What follows is an enchanting exchange between two lovers unwilling to part company: Romeo says he hears the lark, the bird that sings in the morning, and Juliet pulls him back to bed, arguing that it is the nightingale, which sings in the night. The scene is achingly sweet in part because their happiness is so pure, and in part because we know it is the only moment of true happiness that they will ever get to experience. The scene makes the audience believe that their romance is truly special, and it breaks our hearts when it ends.

In one of the most haunting visions of love lost, *Casablanca* (1942) tells the story of Rick (Humphrey Bogart) and Ilsa (Ingrid Bergman), two lovers who lost each other during the early years of WWII. In a flashback, we see they were lovers in Paris. Wrapped in each other's arms, Rick and Ilsa sip champagne and exchange kisses. It is the very image of heaven — until the Nazis begin their march through Paris. In defiance, Rick and Ilsa make a plan to escape to America together, but just before Ilsa is set to meet Rick at the train station, she learns that the husband she thought was dead is very much alive and needs her help. She leaves Rick waiting alone at the terminal. Many years later, when Rick and Ilsa meet again, they find

Casablanca, © 1942 Warner Bros., All Rights Reserved.

a way to recover some part of their love despite the fact that they can never be together. "We'll always have Paris," Rick says as he parts with Ilsa for the last time. The romance of that magical moment depends on the audience knowing that even though they can't be together, for one blissful moment in Paris, they achieved absolute perfection in their love.

FINAL DOOM

More than anything else, the key to the love story in *Romeo and Juliet* is the fact that it ends. This seems counterintuitive, since many romances end "happily ever after." But in truth, we are hardly ever shown that "happily ever after" — the narrative cuts out after they kiss and promise to love each other forever. Why? Because we all know that after forty years of marriage, things are hardly ever as perfect as they were at the beginning. One way to be sure that you'll never find out what it means to get old and tired of each other is to end the romance at its apex, which is exactly what *Romeo and Juliet* does.

At the end of *Romeo and Juliet*, the two lovers put into motion a scheme to outwit their parents and elope. But the plan goes awry when Juliet's letter to Romeo is lost. He returns from exile, believing Juliet is dead. What follows is one of the most tragic scenes ever written. Breaking into Juliet's tomb, Romeo sobs over her seemingly dead body. He can't believe that she's gone — her lips are still red, her cheeks rosy. For one moment, the audience believes Romeo might realize Juliet isn't really dead, only drugged to appear so, but he doesn't. Instead, Romeo drinks the poison, his final words echoing in the dark: "Thus with a kiss I die." Waking too late, Juliet finds Romeo dead at her side. Overcome with grief and eager to join her love, she kills herself.

Their deaths at the end of the play are shocking. If the letter hadn't gone astray, if the Friar had found Romeo first, if Juliet had woken up just a moment earlier — it all seems so unfair. How could a slight miscalculation of fate lead to such complete doom? The entire play seems designed to evoke a visceral emotional reaction to the injustice of Romeo and Juliet's untimely deaths. And yet, the story could not have ended any other way. The play offers us a vision of love doomed by fate, a love too perfect for this world, a love never diminished by the ravages of time. Its doom is what makes their love perfect.

Atonement (2007) features the ill-fated love story of upper-class Cecilia (Keira Knightley) and the servant's son, Robbie (James McAvoy). Despite the prohibitions against their romance, they fall in love. But trouble arises when Briony (Saoirse Ronan), Cecilia's younger sister, spies Cecilia and Robbie having sex. Briony accuses Robbie of raping both her sister and a house guest named Lola. Robbie is imprisoned, only to be released for duty in WWI. In the haunting final sequence of the movie, Briony tells us that Robbie died of septicemia at Dunkirk, and that Cecilia died a bomb victim in London. Because of Briony's lie, the two lovers never have a chance to be together. It is cruel doom. Their chance at happiness may be gone, but, like Romeo and Juliet's, their love will always be perfect.

KEY POINTS TO REMEMBER

† Having your characters be attracted to "forbidden fruit" not only rings true for readers, it also adds an element of thrill by introducing a natural obstacle to the romance.

† Watching the lovers enjoy a glimpse of paradise is utterly intoxicating for the audience, and it is a necessary part of building a compelling romance.

† More than anything else, the key to romance is the fact that it ends, either by separating the lovers or by cutting to "...and they lived happily ever after."

MOVIES TO WATCH

Casablanca (1942)
Titanic (1997)
Atonement (2007)

EXERCISES

1. Imagine yourself into a *Romeo and Juliet* scenario. Who would your friends and loved ones absolutely hate to see you with? Write one paragraph on how you two might fall in love and get together.

2. Think back to the first time you were in love. What was your glimpse of paradise? How might you recreate those blissful moments cinematically?

3. Imagine the perfect romance. Now think of all the forces that could destroy it. Who are the two characters in love? Who or what is keeping them apart, and why? How is their love demolished in the end?

Chapter Eighteen

ABSOLUTE GENIUS: SHAKESPEARE'S SOURCES OF INSPIRATION.

SHAKESPEARE IS GENERALLY REGARDED as the most uniquely gifted writer of all time — one whose universal creative genius transcends barriers of language, culture, time, and place. Around the world, his work is prized for its exceptional inventiveness and originality.

Many writers have wondered how Shakespeare came up with so many wonderful stories. What was his source of inspiration? Where did he find his ideas? What was his secret?

The truth is shocking. Shakespeare *did* have sources of inspiration, but few of Shakespeare's stories are "original" in our sense of the word. In fact, only two of Shakespeare's thirty-eight plays have no known source. The rest were stolen — that's right, *stolen* — from specific, identifiable sources. In other words, scholars actually have a very good idea of where Shakespeare got his inspiration from, as we are about to learn here.

CANNIBALIZE OTHER PEOPLE'S WORK

Almost every single work Shakespeare wrote was written first by someone else. *Othello*, for instance, is taken directly from Giraldi Cinthio's *Hecatommithi*, which was published in England in 1584. Shakespeare changes the original source material in that he promotes the Moor to captain of the army and ennobles him to create the first black tragic hero in Western literature, but the story is essentially the same. Likewise, *Hamlet* is based on a Norse legend of Amleth that was re-told in a poem by French author Francois de Belleforest in

1559, and again, the story was fundamentally the same as the source text. *The Merchant of Venice* was based on the 14th-century tale *Il Pecorone* by Giovanni Fiorentino, and *The Winter's Tale* was based on Robert Greene's *Pandosto* (1588). The list could go on. With the exception of *The Tempest* and *Love's Labor's Lost*, Shakespeare's plays were clearly and obviously based on the work of someone else.

Of course, in Shakespeare's day, this approach to storytelling was not only accepted, it was downright common. Many authors of the time based their stories on the work of someone else. But if you believe that artists have moved past this practice, then you haven't been out to the movies lately — only in Hollywood, they call them "remakes," "adaptations," "reboots," and "homages." At any given time, half of the movies out at theatres fit into one of these categories.

Both then and now, artists have used one another's work and drawn inspiration from each other. Shakespeare knew it was a powerful tool, and he wasn't afraid to use it. Of course, if you read both the source text and Shakespeare, what you'll notice is that Shakespeare's work is far superior. He always made the work his own, and he invariably improved the story. The lesson is clear: don't be afraid to cannibalize other people's work, but always make sure you offer your own spin on the story.

REWORK FAMOUS LEGENDS, MYTHS, AND FOLK TALES

When Shakespeare wasn't busy cannibalizing the work of others, he looked to legends, myths, and folk tales for inspiration. This was certainly the case with *Romeo and Juliet*. Stories of aristocratic lovers separated by family disapproval were common in medieval folk tales. Shakespeare must have known was that the tale would make a good play — and he was right.

In Hollywood, myths, legends, and folk tales are popular resources for creating new franchises. *Thor* (2011) revamped an ancient Norse legend; *Snow White and The Huntsman* (2012) told the famous fairy tale in an entirely new way; *Clash of the Titans* (2010) took classical mythology to a whole new level. Every single one of these movies took creative license with familiar material and proved to be extraordinarily successful at the box office. Both in

Shakespeare's time and in modern Hollywood, legends, myths, and folk tales are a rich source of inspiration.

Thor, © 2011 Paramount, All Rights Reserved.

RAID THE ANNALS OF HISTORY

One of Shakespeare's favorite places to look for inspiration was Holinshed's *Chronicles* (1577). In it, he found tales of murder, revenge, power, and betrayal, and all from the annals of history. In fact, Shakespeare was so captivated by history, he wrote fifteen plays — one third of the total attributed to him — on the matter. Some of his most enduring classics are history plays: *King Lear, Richard III, Macbeth,* and *Henry V,* to name a few.

As with famous tales and cannibalizing other people's work, history remains a popular source of inspiration for writers and artists to this day. Some of the highest-grossing films of all time, such as *Titanic* (1997) and *Gladiator* (2000), were fictional stories based on historical events. The annals of history are a treasure trove of spellbinding tales and thrilling characters — all waiting to be raided by a new crop of creatives.

SHAMELESSLY EXPLOIT THE NEWS

As everyone knows, truth is sometimes stranger than fiction. There's no place better than the news to find strange truths — its sordid and steamy details are a rich source of inspiration for writers looking for fresh ground.

Shakespeare certainly knew how to use current events to boost the excitement in his stories. *King Lear*, for instance, is ostensibly based on historical events. But there was also a famous and wildly controversial case in 1603 of a doddering old gentleman named Sir Brian Annesly who had three daughters, two of whom tried to have the old man declared legally insane. The youngest daughter, Cordell, protested vehemently on her father's behalf. Her name is suspiciously close to Cordelia, a link that Shakespeare possibly intended to make. Regardless of what Shakespeare's intentions were, *King Lear* turned out to be one of his more popular plays on the stage — due in part, no doubt, to its references to current events.

Popular recent movies like *The Blind Side* (2009), *The Social Network* (2010), *Moneyball* (2011), *Argo* (2012), and *Zero Dark Thirty* (2012) draw heavily on real events, even sometimes earning a title card that reads "based on a true story" or "inspired by real events." Recounting details from unusual or controversial true stories can heighten a film's immediacy and the audience's emotional connection.

KEEP IT PERSONAL

Last but not least, we have the old stand-by: draw on your personal experience. The more painful that experience, the better. The advice may seem old hat, but that doesn't mean that it isn't good advice.

We can't be certain if Shakespeare drew on personal experience. Scholars know very little about Shakespeare's life, but one of the few details that has survived involves his children. Shakespeare had a girl, Susanna, and twins, Judith and Hamnet. Hamnet died of unknown causes in 1596 when he was just eleven years old. It seems safe to speculate that Shakespeare was deeply saddened by the death of his only son, not least because three years later, Shakespeare named his best and most brilliant character, Hamlet, after that child. It's more than possible that Shakespeare poured his grief into this play. The result, as we all know, was a timeless masterpiece.

As writers, we instinctively understand that personal experience is absolutely fundamental to our writing. This is a lesson Shakespeare undoubtedly knew: use your personal experience — it will always be your richest source of inspiration.

KEY POINTS TO REMEMBER

† Don't be afraid to cannibalize other people's work, but always make sure you offer your own spin on the story.

† Both in Shakespeare's time and in modern Hollywood, legends, myths, and folk tales offer a wealth of inspiration.

† The annals of history are a treasure trove of spellbinding stories and thrilling characters, all waiting to be raided by a new crop of creatives.

† There's no place better place to find sordid and steamy stories than the news.

† Draw on your personal experience — it will always be your richest store of inspiration.

EXERCISES

1. Ongoing exercise. Start building a file filled with interesting news items. Go through the file once a month and create a one-page outline for a story from one of your collected items.

2. Start a second file filled with images that you find evocative. Why do the images inspire you? Could they be a setting for a particular scene? Do they evoke a mood or tone you find appealing? Could you create a story from one of the images?

3. List out all of your favorite folk tales, legends, myths, historical figures, and old stories that have passed into the public domain. Would any of them make for a good screenplay? Outline a story for your top three candidates.

Chapter Nineteen

WHY SHAKESPEARE'S STORIES STAND THE TEST OF TIME.

SHAKESPEARE'S PLAYS WERE WRITTEN hundreds of years ago. Since that time, thousands of masterpieces — plays, novels, and short stories — have been penned and published. Yet, despite all the competition, Shakespeare is still cited as the greatest writer who ever lived. Shakespeare's plays are, of course, filled with good stories, good characters, and good dialogue, but so are many of the great works produced in the last five hundred years. What makes Shakespeare so special? What makes his work different? Why have his stories managed to stand the test of time?

INNOVATE

If we could think of one thing that defines great masters of art, it would probably be that they are innovators. They are the pioneers of the imagination, giving audiences something they've never heard, seen, or read before.

Although nearly all of his works were based on prior works, Shakespeare was nonetheless a committed innovator. In *Romeo and Juliet*, for instance, he buried a complete sonnet in the first spoken exchange between Romeo and Juliet. As they trade lines, the sonnet progresses to its climax, and they kiss. It is both poetic and romantic, unlike anything that had been done before. In *King Lear*, Shakespeare builds the concept of the play into the form. The play is structured like an avalanche: it starts at a high point of the action and plummets into an abyss. It's downward spiral mirrors the actions and emotions of Lear as he marches toward death. No other play in Shakespeare's canon is structured this way — it was completely unique for its time. In almost every play he wrote, Shakespeare offered the audience satisfying and intriguing innovations in character, language, and dramatic structure.

Innovators would seem common among Hollywood types, but they are actually few and far between. When they do appear — Alfred Hitchcock, Billy Wilder, Orson Welles — they make a splash. This is certainly true of Quentin Tarantino. His groundbreaking *Pulp Fiction* (1994), noted for its non-linear storyline that jumps forward and backward in time, was hailed by movie critic Gene Siskel as a challenge to the "ossification of American movies with their brutal formulas," and Roger Ebert told the *Chicago Sun-Times* that the movie was "so well-written in a scruffy, fanzine way that you want to rub noses in it — the noses of those zombie writers who take 'screenwriting' classes that teach them the formulas for 'hit films.'" Years later, Richard Corliss of *Time* called the movie a cultural event, citing it as "(unquestionably) the most influential American movie of the '90s." Tarantino broke the mold with this film — and he was rewarded with a place in history.

Pulp Fiction, © 1994 Miramax, All Rights Reserved.

GO FOR THE ETERNAL

Shakespeare's work includes comedies, romances, histories, and tragedies. The plays are diverse and unpredictable in both their conception and execution. Yet, each one of his plays touches on a theme rooted in eternal human conflicts and desires. In *Othello*, it's jealousy. In *Macbeth*, it's ambition. In *Romeo and Juliet*, it's love. In *Julius Caesar*, it's betrayal. Love, family, power, war — these are the issues Shakespeare addresses. Shakespeare never goes for the small story; he always goes for the timeless. His plays touch a nerve not because they are topical or fresh but rather because they answer a human need to hear stories that have always, and will always, be told. The stories allow us to feel our way through eternal questions of why we are here and why it matters.

At their best, movies address eternal themes and look to answer eternal questions. This is certainly one of the reasons why *Citizen Kane* (1941) is consistently listed as the best movie ever made. It is a moving story of an ambitious man who, though he has had everything in life, dies sad and alone, repeating the word "Rosebud" like a prayer. We learn in a series of flashbacks that "Rosebud" was the name of his sled — his favorite toy, in the happy days before the goldmine was discovered on his mother's property and he was sent away for a proper education. Through the course of the movie, "Rosebud" comes to symbolize what Kane lost when he became wealthy: love and family. It is a powerful message of loss — one that reaches for answers to eternal human pain and conflict.

MAKE IT POETIC

Human beings have always felt the need to express themselves, beginning with cave drawings of buffalo and spears. The same impulse moves through current poetry, drama, music, and dance. We *need* art — it is a fundamental part of human existence.

Shakespeare answers this need with gorgeous, poetic language in his plays. His language engages the imagination, expands our understanding of ourselves and others, and tickles the ear with beauty. The poetry of his language is stunning — so much so that his words have come to permeate our culture. How many of us have heard of the "green-eyed monster"? Or "all that glitters is not gold"? Or "forever and a day"? Or "dead as a doornail"? Or "kill them with kindness"? Or "one fell swoop"? Or "bated breath"? Or "it's all Greek to me"? The list could go on. Shakespeare is credited with coining thousands of words and phrases, many of which are still popular today. Shakespeare's poetic language looms large in our collective imagination — it is essential to how we remember him. Without that poetry, would Shakespeare's work be more than a faint memory?

The fashion in current screenwriting books is to tell you that dialogue is secondary — that all that really matters is plot. But if you've ever spent time with movie buffs, you know that dialogue is incredibly important: movie buffs memorize long sections of dialogue, repeating it in reverent tones as if they were reciting scripture. Take *Star Wars* (1977), for instance. The movie was a big budget action flick, where the quality of the dialogue would theoretically be less important, and yet the movie is filled with quotable moments. In the years since it first appeared, *Star Wars* has inspired legions of fans who remember every single word spoken in the movie. Dialogue is absolutely one of the most important elements in creating a movie masterpiece. Not all movies need good dialogue, but all masterpieces have great dialogue. We *need* the poetry; we *need* the art.

KEY POINTS TO REMEMBER

† Use your work to innovate and pioneer.

† Go for stories and themes rooted in eternal human conflicts and desires.

† Despite what many screenwriting books will tell you, dialogue is absolutely one of the more important elements of creating a masterpiece.

MOVIES TO WATCH

Citizen Kane (1941)
Star Wars (1977)
Pulp Fiction (1994)

EXERCISES

1.   Think of your favorite movie. Re-tell that movie in a new way. You can make it non-linear, jumping forward and backward in

time; or you could tell it backwards, starting with the climax and moving toward the beginning; or you could take a minor character and tell the story from their point of view.

2. Think of a favorite phrase or line of dialogue from a movie you love. Now rewrite the scene with a catch phrase of your own.

3. Re-watch your favorite movie. What scene is your favorite? Does it contain memorable dialogue? What is it about the dialogue that appeals to you?

PART III

FINAL
THOUGHTS

Chapter Twenty

SHAKESPEARE'S GREATEST LESSON: BREAK THE RULES.

THIS BOOK HAS REVIEWED FIFTEEN of Shakespeare's best plays and broken them down into practical writing lessons. We've dissected Shakespeare's most inspiring heroes and terrifying supervillains, we've discovered how to create a classic drama that stands the test of time, we've combed through Shakespeare's funniest comedies for tips and tricks, and we've sifted through dozens of the greatest films ever made to see what makes them extraordinary. But the most important lesson you can take away from the book is this: break the rules.

If nothing else, Shakespeare was a rule breaker. As famed critic A. C. Bradley once pointed out, Shakespeare steadfastly refused to obey the rules of tragedy set out by Aristotle. His plays are devoid of a single, overarching theme; they produce a medley of characters that can't be reduced to types; and they vary widely in length. In addition, the plays are all structured differently. Not even the dialogue is uniform: some is in verse, some in prose. There is nothing predictable or formulaic about anything Shakespeare wrote.

Shakespeare was a maverick. Instead of adhering to formulas, Shakespeare made every single play exactly what it needed to be without worrying about whether or not it broke the rules. This is what makes Shakespeare special: both his disregard for the establishment and his capacity for making each play perfect in its own right. Every play is utterly unique.

What Shakespeare ultimately teaches us is to not worry if your story fits into typical formulas. Do whatever you have to do to make your story right. If you need to, break the rules of today — just as Shakespeare broke the rules of the sixteenth century.

In other words, be the new Shakespeare. Shakespeare would be the first to applaud.

SUMMARIES OF THE GREAT PLAYS

Richard III (1593)
Wretched and malformed, both inside and out, Richard ruthlessly murders everyone who stands between him and the throne — only to end up losing everything.

The Taming of the Shrew (1593-1594)
In this precursor to the romantic comedy, pig-headed Petruchio "tames" his petulant wife Kate, and everyone lives happily ever after.

Romeo and Juliet (1594)
Often cited as the most romantic story ever told, *Romeo and Juliet* tells of two young lovers who are separated by a family feud — but will live forever together in death.

A Midsummer Night's Dream (1595)
In this whimsical farce, two love-sick couples escape to the forest — only to get caught up in a merry, magical war between the fairies.

The Merchant of Venice (1596)
Jewish moneylender Shylock tries to recover a bad loan to two feckless Gentiles by literally carving up a "pound of flesh" in this extremely dark comedy.

Much Ado About Nothing (1598)
When Claudio falls for Hero, his best friend Benedick is disgusted. So Claudio plays a trick on Benedick — making him fall in love with his arch-enemy, Beatrice. The fun and games end when Hero is accused of cheating on Claudio, but all's well that ends well: the truth comes out, and everyone gets married.

Henry V (1599)
In this coming-of-age tale, Henry proves he has what it takes to be one of the best kings England has ever known when he and his rag-tag group of soldiers defeat a massive French army.

Julius Caesar (1599)
The play offers a behind-the-scenes look at how a bloodthirsty group of conspirators murdered one of the greatest leaders the world has ever known.

Hamlet (1600)
In this cerebral tale of betrayal and revenge, Hamlet learns that his Uncle Claudius murdered his father, married his mother, and stole the kingship. It's up to Hamlet to set it right, but will he be able to do it? Blood and gore finish off this monumental masterpiece.

Othello (1602-1603)
Cold-hearted Iago befriends Othello, a powerful black military leader, only to prey on Othello's jealousy and drive him to murder his beloved wife, Desdemona.

King Lear (1605)
A brutal play filled with cruelty and disasters, *King Lear* is the tale of a father who gives up his kingdom to his three daughters — then gives up his mind. By the end Lear is a madman, naked in a storm, alone and dying.

Macbeth (1606)
In this blood-soaked supernatural thriller, three witches' prophecies drive Macbeth and his wife to murder the king and take over the throne of Scotland.

Antony and Cleopatra (1607-1608)
Hopelessly in love with one of the most enchanting women the world has ever known, Antony struggles to balance love and war, but ends up sacrificing everything — including his life.

The Winter's Tale (1609)

In this strange and gloomy tale, jealous husband Leontes accuses his wife of cheating on him with his best friend and lying about who the father is of their newborn child — then he tries to have them all killed. Leontes pines for his family for sixteen years, then in a bizarre twist, discovers sixteen years later that his wife and child are still alive... and forgive him.

CREDITS FOR
REFERENCED MOVIES

All About Eve (1950), written by Joseph L. Mankiewicz, from a story by Mary Orr; directed by Joseph L. Mankiewicz.

Annie Hall (1977), written by Woody Allen and Marshall Brickman; directed by Woody Allen.

American Beauty (1990), written by Alan Ball; directed by Sam Mendes.

American History X (1998), written by David McKenna; directed by Tony Kaye

Apocalypse Now (1979), written by John Milius and Francis Coppola, from a novel by Joseph Conrad; directed Francis Coppola.

The Artist (2011), written and directed by Michel Hazanavicius.

Atonement (2007), written by Christopher Hampton, from the novel by Ian McEwen; directed by Joe Wright.

Being There (1979), written by Jerzy Kosinski from his novel; directed by Hal Ashby.

Black Swan (2010), written by Mark Heyman, Andres Heinz, and John McLaughlin; directed by Darren Aronofsky.

Bonnie and Clyde (1967), written by David Newman and Robert Benton; directed by Arthur Penn.

Bringing Up Baby (1938), written by Dudley Nichols and Hagar Wilde, from a story by Hagar Wilde; directed by Howard Hawks.

Casablanca (1942), written by Julius J. Epstein, Philip G. Epstein, and Howard Koch, from a play by Murray Burnet and Joan Allison; directed by Michael Curtiz.

Citizen Kane (1941), written by Herman J. Mankiewicz and Orson Welles; directed by Orson Welles.

The Curious Case of Benjamin Button (2008), written by Eric Roth and Robin Swicord, from a story by F. Scott Fitzgerald; directed by David Fincher.

The Dark Knight (2008), written by Jonathan Nolan and Christopher Nolan; directed by Christopher Nolan.

The Departed (2006), written by William Monahan, from a screenplay by Alan Mak and Felix Chong; directed by Martin Scorsese.

Elf (2003), written by David Berenbaum; directed by Jon Favreau.

The Empire Strikes Back (1980), written by Leigh Brackett and Lawrence Kasdan, story by George Lucas; directed by George Lucas.

Extremely Loud & Incredibly Close (2011), written by Eric Roth, from the novel by Jonathan Safran Foer; directed by Stephen Daldry.

The Godfather (1972), written by Francis Ford Coppola and Mario Puzo, from the novel by Mario Puzo; directed by Francis Ford Coppola.

The Godfather: Part II (1974), written by Francis Ford Coppola and Mario Puzo, from the novel by Mario Puzo; directed by Francis Ford Coppola.

The Godfather: Part III (1990), written by Francis Ford Coppola and Mario Puzo, from the novel by Mario Puzo; directed by Francis Ford Coppola.

Good Will Hunting (1997), written by Matt Damon and Ben Affleck; directed by Gus Van Sant.

Groundhog Day (1993), written by Danny Rubin and Harold Ramis; directed by Harold Ramis.

The Hunger Games (2012), written by Gary Ross, Suzanne Collins, and Billy Ray, from the novel by Suzanne Collins; directed by Gary Ross.

Iron Man (2008), written by Mark Fergus, Hawk Ostby, Art Marcum, and Matt Holloway; directed by Jon Favreau.

L.A. Confidential (1997), written by Brian Helgeland and Curtis Hanson, from the novel by James Ellroy; directed by Curtis Hanson.

Lawrence of Arabia (1962), written by Robert Bolt and Michael Wilson; directed by David Lean.

Léon: The Professional (1994), written and directed by Luc Besson.

Life is Beautiful (1998), written by Vincenzo Cerami and Roberto Benigni; directed by Roberto Benigni.

Megamind (2010), written by Alan J. Schoolcraft and Brent Simons; directed by Tom McGrath.

Misery (1990), written by William Goldman, from the novel by Stephen King; directed by Rob Reiner.

On The Waterfront (1954), written by Budd Schulberg; directed by Elia Kazan.

Ordinary People (1980), written by Alvin Sargent; directed by Robert Redford.

Pulp Fiction (1994), written by Quentin Tarantino and Roger Avary; directed by Quentin Tarantino.

Rebel Without a Cause (1955), written by Stewart Stern and Irving Shulman, story by Nicholas Ray; directed by Nicholas Ray.

Rocky (1976), written by Sylvester Stallone; directed by John G. Avildsen.

Scarface (1983), written by Oliver Stone, from a screenplay by Howard Hawks and Ben Hecht and a novel by Armitage Trail; directed by Brian De Palma.

Serpico (1973), written by Waldo Salt and Norman Wexler, from the novel by Peter Maas; directed by Sidney Lumet.

Shadow of a Doubt (1943), written by Thornton Wilder, Sally Benson, Alma Reville, story by Gordon McDonell; directed by Alfred Hitchcock.

The Shining (1980), written by Stanley Kubrick and Diane Johnson, from the novel by Stephen King; directed by Stanley Kubrick.

The Silence of the Lambs (1991), written by Ted Tally, from the novel by Thomas Harris; directed by Jonathan Demme.

Star Wars (1977), written and directed by George Lucas.

Sunset Boulevard (1950), written by Charles Brackett, Billy Wilder, D.M. Marshman Jr.; directed by Billy Wilder.

There Will Be Blood (2007), written by Paul Thomas Anderson, from the novel by Upton Sinclair; directed by Paul Thomas Anderson.

There's Something About Mary (1998), written by Ed Decter, John J. Strauss, Peter Farrelly, Bobby Farrelly, story by Ed Decter and John J. Strauss; directed by Bobby Farrelly and Peter Farrelly.

Thor (2011), written by Ashley Miller, Zack Stentz, and Don Payne, story by J. Michael Straczynski and Mark Protosevich; directed by Kenneth Branagh.

300 (2006), written by Zack Snyder, Kurt Johnstad, and Michael B. Gordon, from the graphic novel by Frank Miller and Lynn Varley; directed by Zack Snyder.

3:10 to Yuma (2007), written by Halstead Welles, Michael Brandt, and Derek Haas, from a story by Elmore Leonard; directed by James Mangold.

Titanic (1997), written and directed by James Cameron.

Top Gun (1986), written by Jim Cash and Jack Epps Jr., from an article by Ehud Yonay; directed by Tony Scott.

Training Day (2001), written by David Ayer; directed by Antoine Fuqua

Wall Street (1987), written by Stanley Weiser and Oliver Stone; directed by Oliver Stone.

Wedding Crashers (2005), written by Steve Faber and Bob Fisher; directed by David Dobkin.

When Harry Met Sally... (1989), written by Nora Ephron; directed by Rob Reiner.

ABOUT THE AUTHOR

J. M. EVENSON received a Ph.D. in Renaissance literature from the University of Michigan and an M.F.A. from UCLA's famed School of Theater, Film and Television. At UCLA, she was awarded the Harmony Gold Screenwriting Prize and the Women In Film Eleanor Perry Writing Award and won top honors at the UCLA Showcase Screenwriting Contest. As a writer in L.A., she has worked with a variety of studios and production houses, from DreamWorks to Focus Features. An award-winning teacher of Shakespeare, composition, and film, Evenson currently teaches at Pepperdine University in Malibu, California.

J. M. Evenson offers consulting, lectures, and workshops.
For more information, please contact:
shakespeareforscreenwriters@gmail.com

{ THE MYTH OF MWP }

In a dark time, a light bringer came along, leading the curious and the frustrated to clarity and empowerment. It took the well-guarded secrets out of the hands of the few and made them available to all. It spread a spirit of openness and creative freedom, and built a storehouse of knowledge dedicated to the betterment of the arts.

The essence of the Michael Wiese Productions (MWP) is empowering people who have the burning desire to express themselves creatively. We help them realize their dreams by putting the tools in their hands. We demystify the sometimes secretive worlds of screenwriting, directing, acting, producing, film financing, and other media crafts.

By doing so, we hope to bring forth a realization of 'conscious media' which we define as being positively charged, emphasizing hope and affirming positive values like trust, cooperation, self-empowerment, freedom, and love. Grounded in the deep roots of myth, it aims to be healing both for those who make the art and those who encounter it. It hopes to be transformative for people, opening doors to new possibilities and pulling back veils to reveal hidden worlds.

MWP has built a storehouse of knowledge unequaled in the world, for no other publisher has so many titles on the media arts. Please visit www.mwp.com where you will find many free resources and a 25% discount on our books. Sign up and become part of the wider creative community!

Onward and upward,

Michael Wiese
Publisher/Filmmaker